RAIL CENTRES:
SHREWSBURY

RAIL CENTRES:
SHREWSBURY

RICHARD K. MORRISS

Nottingham

Booklaw Publications

Acknowledgements

Books of this sort would be impossible to write without the help and enthusiasm of a great many people. I would like to thank the local staff of British Rail, in particular Mr Merrick Roocroft (Area Manager), Mr Jack Beard, Mr Bernard Hitch and Mr Frank Smith (Manager, Hookagate) as well as all the railwaymen I met during the research for the book. Mr Tony Carr and his staff at the Local Studies Library in Shrewsbury were as helpful and enthusiastic as ever, and so were the staff at the County Records Office, Shrewsbury, the Birmingham Reference Library, and the Public Records Office at Kew. Thanks also must go to Mr L. R. H. Coney (Superintendent, HQ Army Dept Railway Staff), Mr Russel Mulford (Shropshire Railway Society), Mr W. Lyons (Severn-Trent Water Authority), Mr John L. Smith (Lens of Sutton), Mr G. Dudley Whitworth and Mr Geoff Williams (London & North Western Railway Society), Mr Richard Keen (Welsh Industrial & Maritime Museum), Mr Len Davies, H. Tempest (Cardiff) Ltd, Perkins Engines (Shrewsbury), and many others.

A very special thanks goes to Mr Peter Clay and Mr Graham Vincent for their help with detailed notes and fascinating photographs, and Mrs Joan Twiselton for technical assistance and a great deal of encouragement. Finally, thanks to all those friends and relations who kept me going — especially to Ruth, for her gentle persuasion.

Richard K. Morriss

First published 1986
by Ian Allan Ltd

©Ian Allan Ltd 1986

This edition published 2004 by Booklaw Publications
382, Carlton Hill, Nottingham NG4 1JA

ISBN 1-901945-20-0

Printed by
The Amadeus Press, Cleckheaton, West Yorkshire

Bibliography

Ahrons, E. L. *Locomotive and train working in the latter part of the nineteenth century*

Allen, C. J. *Titled Trains of the Western*

Baughan, P. E. *Regional History of the Railways of Great Britain; Vol 11: North and Mid-Wales*

Bennet, A. R. *The Chronicles of Boulton's Sidings*

Christiansen, R. and Miller, R. W. *The Cambrian Railways — Vols I and II*

McDermot, E. T. *History of the Great Western Railway* — Vols I and II

Morriss, R. K. *Railways of Shropshire*

Neele, G. P. *Railway Reminiscences*

Nock, O. S. *History of the Great Western Railway — Vol III*

Nock, O. S. *The Premier Line — The Story of London & North Western Locomotives*

Railway Correspondence & Travel Society *Locomotives of the Great Western* (several volumes)

Rolt, L. T. C. *Red For Danger*

Shropshire Railway Society. *Shropshire Railways Revisited*

Smith, D. J. *Shrewsbury to Swansea — The Story of the Railway through Central Wales*

Tonks, E. S. *The Shropshire & Montgomeryshire Railway*

Wilson, H. S. *A History of the Travelling Post Offices of Great Britain*

Right:
'Hall' class 4-6-0 No 4976 *Warfield Hall* pulls out of Shrewsbury with a down Hastings-Birkenhead train while '8F' 2-8-0 No 48706 waits for the signal to proceed with a down freight. Waiting at the platform is 'Saint' class 4-6-0 No 2933 *Bibury Court* with the 4.50pm Shrewsbury-Gobowen. The date is 28 August 1952. *Brian Morrison*

Contents

1 Outline History

Shrewsbury has been an important regional centre since the Norman baron Roger de Montgomery chose its easily defended site as the headquarters from which to control the vast tracts of borderland given to him for his part in the Conquest. Lying on hilly ground, the early settlement was almost surrounded by a loop of the River Severn, which acted as a natural moat. In the Middle Ages it became an important market town and trading centre, a place where several strategic roads met; it was also an inland port, for the Severn was navigable as far upstream as the Welsh border up until the mid-19th century. Despite its growth it never was to become an important industrial town, which is probably why the first railway to reach it did not open until the comparatively late date of 1848.

The earliest schemes involving railways routed through Shrewsbury were on a national rather than local scale. The town lies on the direct route between London and Holyhead, which in the early 19th century had become important following the Union with Ireland. This main road was radically rebuilt by Telford after the Napoleonic Wars and for a time Shrewsbury became an important coaching town. With the advent of the railways a rail route to take the Irish traffic attracted considerable interest, but most schemes involved building lines off the new Grand Junction (authorised in 1833) in Cheshire and following the coastal plain of North Wales to reach Anglesey, by-passing Shrewsbury altogether. In 1835 the small Ffestiniog Railway first put forward the idea of an alternative port for the Irish traffic, to be built on the Lleyn Penninsular near Morfa Nevin; in the following year, Charles Vignolles surveyed three routes to this proposed port — Porth Dynlleyn — two of which would have gone through Shrewsbury. Both left the Grand Junction line near Wolverhampton before reaching Shrewsbury by way of the Severn valley and Ironbridge. One then continued westwards towards Welshpool before crossing through and under the Welsh mountains to the coast. The other headed northwards to the Dee valley, following that and other valleys to

Porthmadoc. Nothing came of either proposal because the Admiralty declared the site of the proposed port unsuitable, but the dream of an alternative port to Holyhead was to persist for several decades.

The most obvious route to appeal to local interests was one that would link the town with the growing industrial area of the West Midlands along with the Grand Junction Railway. In 1839 that company's Engineer, Joseph Locke, had surveyed such a route but the idea was shelved. A few years later the Grand Junction was in bitter dispute with its southern neighbour, the London & Birmingham, each company seeing the other as holding an unwelcome monopoly over their respective routes. Under the direction of Mark Huish, its Secretary, the Grand Junction actively encouraged the Great Western Railway in its attempt to create a new route from London to the Midlands by way of the Broad Gauge and Oxford, even though Huish had little love for the Broad Gauge or for the Great Western. In reply the London & Birmingham supported two schemes that would together provide an alternative route from the Midlands to the Mersey and even agreed to lease the first of these, the Shrewsbury, Wolverhampton, Dudley & Birmingham Railway, offering a guaranteed dividend of 4½% and half any surplus profits. Traffic was to be taken on from Shrewsbury by the Shropshire & Cheshire Railway which joined the Chester & Holyhead Railway at Chester. Huish responded by having Locke survey the Shrewsbury-Birmingham route again in 1844 and then backing a rival scheme, the Shrewsbury, Wolverhampton & South Staffs Railway.

The prospect of a Shropshire & Cheshire Railway disturbed the hitherto peaceful progress of the North Wales Mineral Railway, a small concern to link the industrial areas around Wrexham with the railways at Chester. The company saw the planned Shrewsbury-Chester line taking much of the traffic off its as yet unopened railway and so sponsored an alternative scheme — the Shrewsbury, Oswestry & Chester Railway — that would use North Wales Mineral rails north of Ruabon to

reach Chester. In the bitter parliamentary disputes of 1845 this was the only one of the four local schemes to receive the Assent, on 30 June. Just over a year later, on 27 July, the new company was merged with its parent company becoming the Shrewsbury & Chester Railway, the first to reach Shrewsbury.

In the meantime the two rival schemes to build lines to the Midlands lost their respective backers when the Grand Junction and London & Birmingham railways became the major components of the powerful new London & North Western Railway in 1846, under Huish's control. Just before they resumed battle at Westminster in 1846 the two schemes amalgamated and the Assent for the new Shrewsbury & Birmingham Railway was obtained on 3 August. Despite its new title the railway did not actually go to Birmingham. The portion from Wolverhampton was to be built by a new company, the Stour Valley Railway, in which the Shrewsbury & Birmingham, the London & North Western and the Birmingham Canal Co each had a quarter share, the rest coming from public subscription.

On the same day that the Shrewsbury & Birmingham Bill was passed, two other local lines were authorised. The Shrewsbury & Hereford Railway planned to link up with the Newport, Abergavenny & Hereford Railway and so reach the industrial and mining areas of South Wales. It had beaten a rival scheme surveyed by Brunel but financial problems were to delay any start on the line for several years. As its name suggests, the Shropshire Union of Railways & Canals was an ambitious company. Formed by local canal companies to combat the railway threat to their livelihoods it was authorised to raise nearly £5½million with which its engineers, who included Stephenson and Cubitt, were to 'lay out a system of lines of railway' using the existing canal beds where possible 'and making new railways where they thought it necessary'. Altogether the Shropshire Union planned over 155 miles of railway, mostly on the routes of the converted canals, and it also proposed including the Shrewsbury & Birmingham company in the Union. As it was, the only section ever built was a new line from Shrewsbury to Stafford, and this was built jointly with the Birmingham company as far as Wellington.

The first General Meeting of the Shrewsbury, Oswestry & Cheshire company was held in September 1845 and at it Robert Roy was

Above:
Shrewsbury station frontage, April 1982. *Author*

appointed Secretary at a salary of £275 per annum. Work had already started on the line with local businessman Henry Robertson as Engineer, and Thomas Brassey as Contractor. Work was slowed down in the spring of 1846 'due to the uncertain financial climate', but things had improved by the next summer and most of the earthworks were well under way. The main difficulty on the approach to Shrewsbury was the crossing of a former river bed of the Severn just to the north of the town; this marshy land was known locally as the Black Bog, and part of the earthworks collapsed in April 1847. Robertson had to use raft after raft of brushwood held in line by long wooden piles before a sufficiently stable base was obtained on which to raise the tall embankment needed for a level approach to the town.

In the summer of 1848 Robertson was able to report that most of the line was ready and that locomotives were running between Coton Hill, Shrewsbury, and the viaduct at Chirk: he estimated the final cost to be in the region of £15,500 per mile. Despite a five week masons' strike that same summer the line was ready for opening in October. On the morning of

12 October the local dignitaries assembled at the Guild Hall before marching down with band and banners to the as yet unfinished station, which was being built jointly by the four companies building railways to the town. A train had already arrived in the early morning from Chester, but the official inaugural train left just after 10am, half an hour late. It consisted of 39 carriages holding upwards of a thousand passengers hauled by three locomotives, and it was cheered by the trackside along the first mile out of town, and thereafter at every bridge. Once the train reached Chester things began to go wrong. No banquet had been laid on and there was 'neither a biscuit to eat, nor a glass with which one brother corporator could hob nob with another'. In their search for food in Chester itself, over 100 of the party missed the train home and had to catch up later. The return to Shrewsbury was two hours late and was followed by a banquet at the Music Hall and a celebration ball at the Lion Hotel. There was a fireworks display at the Lord Hill monument to round the day off, and a holiday was declared.

As a simple branch line from Chester, the first few months of the new railway were both peaceful and prosperous. The opening of the Shrewsbury & Birmingham line was obviously going to change that as the alternative

Midlands-Mersey line would become a reality. Even before that had happened the two companies had discussed through traffic agreements so as 'to afford additional accommodation to the public . . . and to promote the interests of the shareholders'. The London & North Western Railway was only too aware of this possible threat to its own traffic which it had helped bring about, and so took steps to combat it. In 1847 the company bought the Birmingham Canal Co, thereby getting a majority on the Board of the Stour Valley line. It also leased the Shropshire Union, a move only permitted by the Shrewsbury & Birmingham on the understanding that the London & North Western would not use its new acquisition 'to compete for any traffic which properly belongs to the Shrewsbury & Birmingham'. The Shropshire Union remained theoretically independent until 1922.

William Baker was the Engineer of the joint line from Shrewsbury to Wellington and there were few difficulties on it except for the approach to Shrewsbury, which involved two bridges across the Severn, one by the Joint station, and the other at Preston Boats (now called Belvidere) just outside the town. Here Baker designed a graceful double span bridge, each span being of 101ft, using castings made by the Coalbrookdale Co resting on stone abutments. Tragically one man died in the approach cutting when it collapsed on to him, and two others drowned after falling off the unfinished bridge in 1849.

The wet summer of 1848 hindered work on the Shrewsbury & Birmingham line east of Wellington and Baker invoked clerical wrath for having his men work on Sundays 'in flagrant breach of the Sabbath', but by the time the entire length of the Shropshire Union was ready for opening, the Shrewsbury & Birmingham was only finished as far as Oakengates; the tunnel there was not yet completed. The celebrations for this second line from Shrewsbury were slightly more muted than for the first and took place on 1 June 1849. By November the rest of the Birmingham line was ready to Wolverhampton and on 12 November two suitably named locomotives, *Wrekin* and *Salopian*, hauled the inaugural through-train. The Stour Valley was still not complete and it would be another five years before Shrewsbury & Birmingham trains could run into their rightful destination.

The Railway Mania of 1846 saw many schemes come and go, mostly bizarre and worth little more than the paper on which their glossy prospectuses were written on. One scheme passing through Shrewsbury, the London & Holyhead & Porth Dynnlaen Railway, hoped to raise many millions to construct a new trunk route using 'Pilbrow's Atmospheric Principle'; others were slightly less ambitious. However, in the financial backlash of the mania many worthy railway schemes suffered, amongst them the Shrewsbury & Hereford. At one stage the company had looked like folding, but the persistence of its Engineer, the redoubtable Henry Robertson, and its Chairman, William Ormsby-Gore (one-time Chairman of the Shrewsbury & Chester, the Shrewsbury & Birmingham and the Joint Station Committee as well) kept the company going and in 1850 they had persuaded Brassey to build the line and work it at his own risk once it was opened. Brassey probably agreed simply to keep his well-trained workforce together. Work started in 1850 and despite many steep gradients on the line there were few serious engineering difficulties. The approach to Shrewsbury was on a 700ft long viaduct which crossed the Rea Brook on a 60ft brick skew bridge; 17 other brick arches carried the track to the bridge over the Abbey Foregate, which was designed on the then novel box-girder principle using three 63ft wrought iron girders resting on abutments carrying the tracks 16ft above the road. The ironwork of the bridge was painted a

Below:
The opening of the Shrewsbury & Birmingham Railway 1849.

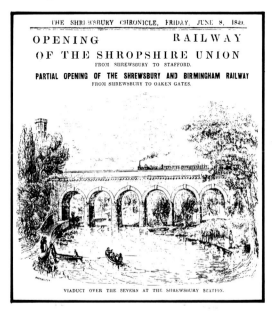

THE SHREWSBURY CHRONICLE, FRIDAY, JUNE 8, 1849.

OPENING RAILWAY
OF THE SHROPSHIRE UNION
FROM SHREWSBURY TO STAFFORD.
PARTIAL OPENING OF THE SHREWSBURY AND BIRMINGHAM RAILWAY
FROM SHREWSBURY TO OAKEN GATES.

VIADUCT OVER THE SEVERN AT THE SHREWSBURY STATION.

dull red to blend in with the nearby Abbey. The viaduct consumed 8,295cu yd of bricks, 7,642cu ft of coping stone and ashlar, and was 35ft high.

The line was opened as far as Ludlow in April 1852, and ready for goods traffic throughout by July; passengers were not taken to Hereford until 6 December 1853. Brassey leased the line and appointed as its manager a young engineer, George Findlay, who later became Manager of the London & North Western.

By the early 1850s Shrewsbury had become a fairly important railway junction; it had also become something of a battleground. Undeterred by the implicit threats of the London & North Western, the two Shrewsbury companies had gone ahead with their traffic agreements between Wolverhampton and Chester, and to make matters worse they agreed to undercut the larger company's passenger fares on the route in October 1849. Huish was enraged and wrote to the two

Secretaries: to Roy he wrote 'I need not say that if you should be unwise enough to encourage such a proceeding it must result in a general fight'. Roy responded to this threat by publishing Huish's letter and cheekily suggesting that Huish had written 'in the hurry of business'. Later he was to write regretting 'that the contest in which we are engaged should have required on your part the suspension of civilities', for once the Shrewsbury & Birmingham line was ready the 'general fight' promised by Huish was always bitter, occasionally violent, extremely costly and very one sided as the London & North Western at that time was the most powerful railway company in the world and led by one of the most ruthless managers in railway history.

Below:
A map of Shrewsbury c1851 showing the early railways.

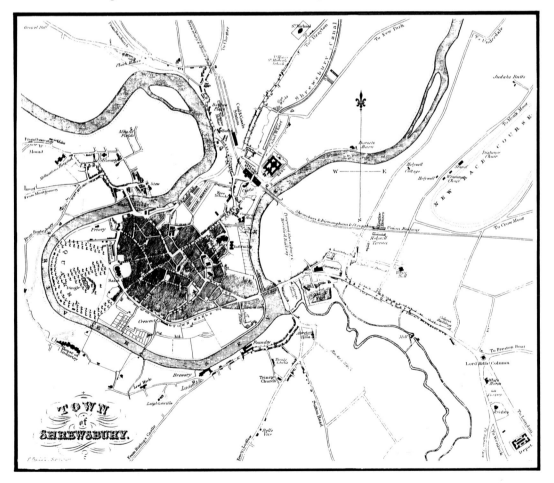

The two Shrewsbury companies' — the 'Fighting Shrewsburies' — route had two distinct disadvantages: at both ends it relied on other railways to reach either the main part of the Midlands or the Mersey, and the London & North Western had managed to obtain control over both these other railways. In the north the Shrewsbury companies relied on the Birkenhead Railway to take their traffic on to the Mersey. The Shrewsbury & Chester actually finished at Saltney Junction just outside Chester and ran into that town's Joint station along the Chester & Holyhead. These running powers were not attacked by Huish who instead relied on the Chairman of the Birkenhead company, James Bancroft, who was in the pay of the London & North Western. With a comfortable majority on the Joint Station Committee at Chester Huish managed to stop all through booking past Wolverhampton by way of the Shrewsbury lines and everything was done to interfere with their through goods and passenger traffic; the

Booking Clerk of the Shrewsbury & Chester was even evicted from the station and the company's timetables and advertisements were torn down. Court Orders were needed to restore the peace.

At the other end of the two companies' through route William Baker, now the Engineer of the Stour Valley, managed to hold up its completion until 1 July 1852, and even then it was not until 4 February 1854 that the Shrewsbury & Birmingham could run trains

Below:
Great Western No 14 (ex-Shrewsbury & Chester No 14). Built by Sharps in July 1848 and withdrawn in December 1885, it was preserved at Wolverhampton before being broken up c1920. *Real Photos*

Bottom:
A rare shot of a Potteries, Shrewsbury & North Wales passenger train at the Abbey station c1872, with ex-LNWR 0-4-2 No 1859. *Real Photos*

along the line into New Street station. The illegal bullying tactics were effective in their way, but far more damaging to the Shrewsbury companies was the re-routing of goods traffic away from the Shrewsbury lines which was subsidised by the London & North Western. At each end of their route the 'Fighting Shrewsburies' were forced to resort to waterborne transport — the Dee at Saltney and the Birmingham Canal from Wolverhampton, a costly and time-consuming arrangement. By the end of 1850 they were beginning to get into severe financial trouble and eventually decided to approach the Great Western for help, which was only too willing to do so as it saw the prospect of the Broad Gauge reaching the Mersey. Accordingly an Agreement was signed on 10 January 1851 with regards to

through traffic between the newly 'Associated Companies', and amalgamation was also promised at a future date. Huish was naturally furious at the prospect of the Great Western competing for the Mersey traffic and set about offering the Shrewsbury companies' shareholders guaranteed dividends from a London & North Western lease of their lines. Civil war broke out in the 'Fighting Shrewsburies' between factions of shareholders for the Great

Western or for the London & North Western, and in the early months of 1851 meeting followed counter-meeting as the two proposals — amalgamation or leasing — were rejected or accepted. Huish supplemented the shareholders of the London & North Western side with workers of that company who would be given shares simply to vote at critical meetings, arriving on special trains from Euston to do so. Alternative Boards were voted in, and at one meeting the Shrewsbury & Birmingham's seal was forged — but even Huish never dared to use it. Ormsby-Gore had to officiate at many of these meetings and during one particularly long and arduous session he pointedly read a book throughout the day before taking out a night cap at 9pm and falling asleep. Once the Great Western's offer of amalgamation had been put in writing,

most genuine opposition to it ceased and despite the attentions of Huish each company agreed to it: the Great Western had almost reached the Mersey. The Birkenhead Railway was still in the hands of Huish for several years and, apart from a brief interlude between October 1851 and December 1852, did as the London & North Western demanded. Although the Shrewsbury & Chester had been given running powers over the Birkenhead, that company retrospectively charged the maximum tolls possible in early 1854 and even had the bailiffs seize the Shrewsbury & Chester's stations for three days in March before the money due was paid; traffic did manage to keep going, though.

Huish still tried to stop the Amalgamation but despite continuing arguments, bitter meetings and constant re-routeing of traffic,

Left:
Many of Webb's failed Compounds ended their short days at Shrewsbury, where they were kept in excellent condition. No 1505 *Richard Arkwright* was the last of the three-cylinder classes to survive, and is seen here entering the station c1905. *Real Photos*

Below:
The aftermath of the mail train disaster of 12 October 1907. *Shropshire Libraries*

Below:
No 2052 *Stephenson* at Coleham, Shrewsbury, after the 1907 crash. Despite the extensive damage, the LNWR repaired the locomotive and it ran for several years afterwards. *Real Photos*

Bottom:
Churchward '43XX' 2-6-0 No 4352 piloting an unidentified 'Saint' 4-6-0 on a North-to-West express just south of Shrewsbury c1917. *Real Photos*

the Shrewsbury boards stood firm. All railway amalgamation was postponed in 1853 and this bitter battle reached its last stage at the start of 1854. The Amalgamation Bill was opposed by the London & North Western, the Shropshire Union, the Newport, Abergavenny & Hereford, the Birkenhead, and the Oxford, Worcester & Wolverhampton; the Shrewsbury & Hereford wisely kept out of things, apart from allowing any one's traffic over its line and once approaching the Shrewsbury companies about the possibility of laying the Broad Gauge over it if the Great Western laid the gauge to the Mersey. The Bill was passed on 7 August, but the dream of the Broad Gauge to the Mersey died with it, as it was specifically prohibited in the Act, which took effect from 1 September. The Shrewsbury companies became the first standard gauge sections of the Great Western, and by 14 November were running into the new Low Level station at Wolverhampton and from there along the mixed gauge line to Snow Hill. The Shrewsbury & Birmingham share of the High Level station was sold to the London & North Western for £80,000.

Initially the Great Western did little to change the way the lines were run as it had no experience of the 'narrow gauge'. The company did re-lay much of the track and began to build new locomotives, but by virtue of its isolation — physical for the few weeks until the Great

Western reached Wolverhampton — from the rest of the system, it became known as the Northern Division with the headquarters in Shrewsbury. This Northern Division soon covered all standard gauge workings from Birmingham to Birkenhead, as the Birkenhead Co was finally acquired jointly by the Great Western and the London & North Western in 1860, and early in 1861 the Divisional headquarters were transferred to Chester.

As part of its tactics against the 'Fighting Shrewsburies' in the early 1850s, the London & North Western had promoted a line from its main junction at Crewe to Shrewsbury. More importantly this was seen as part of a major trunk route to link the northwest of the country with South Wales and its collieries. The Shrewsbury & Crewe Railway was authorised on 20 August 1852 and work progressed quickly. In Shrewsbury the engineers had the same problem with the former river bed of the Severn at Ditherington, but had more problems with the House of Lords which refused to sanction the planned route into the General station — which would have been from the

Below:
An unidentified GWR 4-4-0 heads east from Shrewsbury in November 1918. In the middle distance is the Abbey Foregate goods depot; beyond the second overbridge was the site of Potteries Junction. *Shropshire Libraries*

east after crossing the Severn on an 11-arch bridge near Dorsetts Barn. Rather than terminate in a field outside the town the company agreed to a change in approach and reached the station over the only tight curve in an otherwise well engineered route, joining the Shrewsbury & Chester line at Crewe Junction at the north end of the station. The single line opened on 1 September 1858 and proved so very successful that it had been doubled by 1862.

The idea of a line south from Shrewsbury down the Severn Valley to Worcester by way of Ironbridge had been proposed several times but little was done until 1852 when the Severn Valley Railway got its authorisation on the same day as the Shrewsbury & Crewe. Financial problems delayed any start on the work and the original route, which would have crossed the Severn many times (including once in Shrewsbury next to the proposed Shrewsbury & Crewe bridge), was radically altered and instead of joining the Shrewsbury & Chester line at Coton Hill and having no connection with the General station or any other line, the finished route joined the Shrewsbury & Hereford line at Sutton Bridge and ran in on its rails to the station. Inevitably the Contractor of the line was Brassey, who even put up £30,000 of his own money, and John Fowler was the Engineer: the estimated cost was £13,000 per mile. Rather oddly, the line Brassey was leasing at the time — the Shrewsbury & Hereford — petitioned against the Severn Valley at first yet at the same time allowed its own locomotive Superintendent to build a 44ft steam barge to help in the construction. This was launched at Coleham in September 1858 and the river barge owners who had fought so strongly against the Severn Valley line must have been furious that they couldn't even profit much during its construction. The line was ready by the early summer

of 1861 and unofficial trains ran along it to the Wenlock Olympics in Whit Week with passengers in little more than mineral wagons. The Company left the line to settle as there had been many problems with landslips in the section south of Ironbridge, and the line was finally opened at the end of the following February. The line was worked from the first by the short-lived West Midland Railway, which leased it for 999 years.

For a variety of reasons the Great Western agreed to amalgamate with the West Midland company soon after its formation (as an amalgamation of the Oxford, Worcester & Wolverhampton, the Newport, Abergavenny & Hereford, and the Worcester & Hereford companies in July 1860), a move which worried the Directors of the Shrewsbury & Hereford who saw their line outflanked by the Great Western. To make matters worse Brassey's lease was up for renewal and they faced the prospect of having to fight the competition with no locomotives — they all belonged to Brassey. They approached the London & North Western which quickly agreed to lease a line by which they would have easy access to the areas of South Wales by virtue of the Shrewsbury & Hereford's running powers over the former Newport, Abergavenny & Hereford. The line was prosperous in its own right under Findlay's management, and had been doubled as far as Church Stretton by February 1862, with work on the section to

Below left:
An ex-LSWR 0-6-0 as Shropshire & Montgomeryshire Railway No 6 *Thisbe*. *Ian Allan Library*

Below right:
GWR 'Star' class 4-6-0 No 4025 *Italian Monarch* at Shrewsbury. Named *King Charles* until October 1927, the new name was removed for obvious reasons in June 1940. *Real Photos*

Ludlow well under way by the spring. Huish had been discredited after the disputes with the other Shrewsbury companies and had resigned in 1859; relations had thawed between the Great Western and London & North Western to the extent that the latter tactfully offered the Great Western a share in the lease of the Hereford line. After an uncharacteristic delay and an initial refusal the Great Western agreed and the line was leased equally between the London & North Western on the one hand and the Great Western and West Midland on the other as from 1 July 1862. The Shrewsbury & Hereford bought all the Brassey locomotives and these were divided between the lessees with half going to the London & North Western and half to the Great Western/West Midland partnership. The line was finally vested jointly between the London & North Western and the Great Western in 1870, though it remained nominally independent until 1948.

Shrewsbury had been the natural marketing outlet for large parts of the Welsh borderland for centuries and a rail link between the town and Welshpool was another scheme often considered, but with little actually done. These schemes also hoped to tap the rich mineral potential of the border areas which were particularly rich in good quality limestone and in lead. The Shrewsbury & Welshpool Railway was authorised on 29 July 1856 to link the two towns, together with a branch from Hanwood to Minsterley. A proviso stipulated that the branch had to be ready at the same time as the main line, but its extension through the Rea valley to Bishops Castle was turned down. As it was the branch was ready before the main line, due mainly to repeated failed attempts to tunnel under Middletown Hill which finally broke the original contractor. A local contractor from Shrewsbury, Richard Samuel France, diverted the line around the hill abandoning

the tunnel altogether. The junction for the branch line was at Cruckmeole, just west of Hanwood, and the main line as far as there together with the branch itself was opened on 14 February 1861. The delays to the rest of the main line meant that it was not open throughout until almost a year later with the inaugural train leaving the Joint station at Shrewsbury on 27 January 1862 'without blast of trumpet or roll of drums'. The line actually went as far as Buttington Junction just outside Welshpool, running into that town on the metals of the Oswestry & Newtown Railway (later part of the Cambrian Railways).

Before the line was opened throughout, Shrewsbury had seen its first major railway accident. France lived in Shrewsbury and had a private train to take him to and from the workings around Middletown; as many of his workers also lived in Shrewsbury he allowed them to be carried by the same train in mineral wagons. In the early morning of 23 October 1861 a workers' train carrying about 200 men in six such wagons left the Hereford line at the new junction at Sutton Bridge. After picking up more men near Red Hill the draw bar on one of its wagons separated and caused that wagon and the one behind to leave the tracks and fall down a 6ft embankment. Two of the men who had been sitting on the sides of the wagons were killed, and a third died from his injuries.

The Welshpool line was run from the first by the London & North Western which leased it officially in 1864 and then offered the Great Western a share in it; the line thus became operated jointly by the two companies from the first day of 1865. Initially it was single throughout, but the section as far west as Cruckmeole Junction was doubled by the following June.

The Great Western and London & North Western found themselves in complete control of the local railways, and the various Joint Traffic committees of each of the shared lines and the Joint station were amalgamated into one overall Joint Committee in 1864. For the rest of the century the town enjoyed a period of quiet prosperity from its railways and a steady increase in traffic, both passenger and goods. Each company was also extending its services. After the failure to get the Broad Gauge laid to the Mersey, the Great Western logically decided that the next best thing was to get the Narrow Gauge extended southwards to London. An extension of the gauge to Basingstoke had in any case been a proviso of the Amalgamation Act with the 'Fighting Shrewsburies' in 1854. Once the first standard gauge train ran into Paddington station in August 1861 Shrewsbury was on a major trunk railway between the metropolis and the Mersey. A further important gauge conversion was that of the South Wales Railway in 1872, and the completion of the important 'missing link' in the form of the Pontypool, Caerleon & Newport Railway in 1874 gave the Great Western a single gauge link between South Wales and Birkenhead, meeting the main line from London at Shrewsbury. The opening of the Severn Tunnel in 1886 extended the route south to Bristol and the southwest of England.

In the meantime the London & North Western had been promoting a series of small railways to Swansea through difficult mountain terrain. The whole length of the route was open by 1871 and became known as the Sugar Loaf line from a particular mountain on the way, although it is perhaps better known today as the Central Wales line.

In Shrewsbury itself there were continuous improvements to the goods yards and sidings, and the station was enlarged at the start of the 1860s. To reduce further the congestion at the station, the Joint Committee sanctioned the building of a loop line from the Hereford line just north of the Abbey Foregate bridge to the Wellington line just to the west of Underdale Road. Known as the Abbey Curve this short section of track was opened on 1 May 1867 and although it was a mere 25 chains in length and

Below left:

A Shropshire & Montgomeryshire daily goods train at Meole Brace on 26 July 1940, hauled by ex-LNWR 0-6-0 'Coal Engine' S&MR No 2. This engine later reverted to its old number, 8108, under WD ownership. The S&MR and the Welshpool lines run side by side at this point. *Graham Vincent*

Below right:

World War 2 brought an increase in goods traffic through Shrewsbury and even greater diversity of motive power. Beames 0-8-4T No 7941 hauls a Shrewsbury-Swansea heavy goods near Condover on 24 March 1942. These engines were designed to work heavy coal trains in South Wales. *Peter Clay/LoS*

Above:
Ex-GWR No 4061 *Glastonbury Abbey* about to depart from Shrewsbury with a Chester train in August 1950. A pair of ex-LMS 'Black Fives' is in the background. *Real Photos*

Right:
Shed paraphernalia at Coleham on 9 September 1965. *L. A. Nixon*

had a 5mph speed limit it dramatically eased the burden on the station lines and was especially helpful for through goods from the south to the east. Underdale Road was originally crossed by a level crossing, with a wooden footbridge available for pedestrians. With the increase in traffic using the line there were many complaints to the Joint Committee and in the papers about the crossing gates being locked. The footbridge became dangerous and was even badly damaged by a train in early 1872. It was decided to build a new subway, which was finished later that same year. The only remaining level crossing in the town was, and still is, on the Crewe line at Harlescott, then just a small hamlet on the edge of the town.

While the Joint companies were enjoying a period of peaceful prosperity and increased traffic receipts the only other line to reach the town was seldom to share in such good fortune. Richard France had extensive limestone quarrying interests in the area to the west of the border village of Llanymynech; in

order to get his stone to the main markets — the ironworks of the Midlands — it had to go by way of Oswestry and Gobowen to reach the Shrewsbury & Chester line, or by way of Buttington Junction and the new Welshpool line. He promoted a modest mineral line as a short cut, and the West Shropshire Mineral Railway was authorised, on 29 July 1862, to build a line from near Llanymynech to Westbury on the Welshpool line. France had been involved with several unsuccessful lines linking Shrewsbury with Mid-Wales and with the growing confidence in railway speculation in the early 1860s it was not long before he had obtained new powers to divert the line to a new junction with the Welshpool line at Red Hill, just outside Shrewsbury. He now intended to carry passengers as well as minerals but the running powers from Red Hill

to the Joint (or General) station in Shrewsbury over the Welshpool line were not made mandatory and had to be negotiated. The new concern became the Shrewsbury & North Wales Railway in Acts of 1863 and 1864. Before the line was ready France had formed an alliance with a struggling company trying to link parts of the Stoke-on-Trent area with Shrewsbury, authorised in 1862 as the Shrewsbury & Potteries Junction. This company proposed to join the Crewe line at Battlefield, but again the running powers into the General station had to be negotiated.

Neither the Great Western nor the London & North Western were at all keen to let a rival company interfere with their local monopoly or disrupt their station arrangements, and running powers to the station for both schemes were refused. The London & North Western did offer to take Shrewsbury & North Wales trains into the General station using its locomotives just charging cost price for the service, but France refused what seemed to be a reasonable arrangement. Together the two usurping companies planned an alternative station and the Potteries section was diverted through Shrewsbury to meet the North Wales scheme. Instead of joining the Crewe line at Battlefield the deviation route ran parallel to it until Ditherington before branching off to cross the Severn and then the Wellington line near Sparrow Lane; the line then ran down a cutting near Bell Lane before crossing under the Abbey Foregate road, crossing the Rea Brook and a mill stream, the Severn Valley line and the Hereford line, reaching the Welshpool line in Belle Vue, which it ran alongside before crossing it on the level to meet the Shrewsbury & North Wales at Red Hill. Work on the junction here had actually started but was abandoned once no agreement could be reached with the London & North Western.

By an Act of 1866 the two companies amalgamated to become the grand-sounding Potteries, Shrewsbury & North Wales Railway which had ambitions to provide a direct rail link between the Potteries and the mythical port of Porth Dynnlaen by way of Shrewsbury. As it was, only the portion of the Shrewsbury & North Wales main line between Llanymynech and Red Hill and the Potteries section from there to a junction with the Wellington lines, together with three branch lines, were built, though work did start on the approach embankment to the bridge over the Severn. The company never got anywhere near the Potteries, and only limped over into Wales on two short branches to Nantmawr and to Criggion.

Well-built and optimistically double-tracked, the line opened on 13 August 1866 preceded by a simple announcement in the local papers. By 3 December the line was already in trouble and a creditor called in the Receivers; other notices appeared in local papers advertising the sale of much of the company's stock. With receiver's men on every train the line continued until 21 December when all traffic ceased. It was two years before traffic was restarted. Just why the line was so quickly into difficulties is not hard to see; it had really been planned as a trunk route with little regard to the realities of surviving on the traffic receipts of what was a very sparsely populated rural area. By the time the over-ambitious schemes to reach the Welsh coast had been abandoned most shareholders wanted to sell and most creditors wanted their money. The disappearance of over £1½million in a rural branch line barely 20 miles long is something of a mystery; but Richard France seemed to have been something of a dubious character altogether, and certainly dominated the affairs of the railway to such an extent that it was known locally at the time as 'Mr France's Railway', becoming known by its more common name — 'The Potts' — slightly later. France's business activities were curtailed by a Deed of Arrangement from the Bankruptcy Court in July 1866 but he seems to have carried on for some after that.

On re-opening it would appear that the line was operated as a single track railway, and the second set of rails had gone by 1873. In 1872 the company actually made a profit, having receipts of £9,201 and expenses of £8,182, but this sort of dividend on such a huge outlay was patently unsatisfactory. Despite cost-cutting and reducing fares the company was in deep trouble by the mid-1870s and could not even maintain the line in a safe condition. The Board of Trade became aware of the company's impoverished state and was alarmed at how unsafe the line was becoming, imposing a 25mph speed limit at the start of 1880. Later that same year, it threatened to close the line if certain bridges were not repaired. Some hope came from an unexpected quarter at this time as the Great Northern Railway had built a line to Derby and acquired another to Stafford from Uttoxeter. The company hoped to obtain running powers over the Shropshire Union line to Shrewsbury and from there to reach the Cambrian Railways by way of the ailing 'Potts', thus opening a new trans-Britain trunk route. There was a great deal of opposition from the London & North Western however, and the Bill to obtain running powers to Shrewsbury was dropped on 21 June 1880; a day later, without warning, all traffic on the Potteries, Shrewsbury & North Wales Railway ceased and the line closed for the second time in just 14 years. This time the period of inactivity was to be much longer and despite

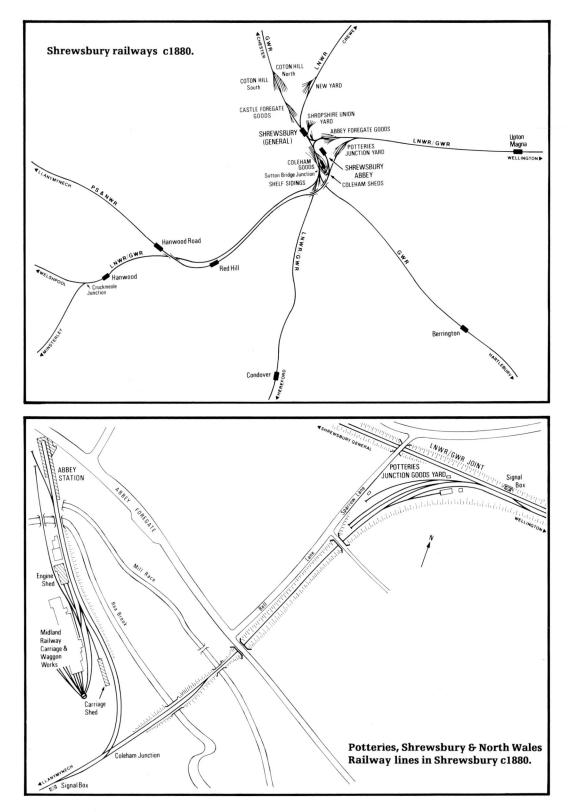

Shrewsbury railways c1880.

CHESTER
GWR
LNWR
CREWE

COTON HILL North
COTON HILL South
NEW YARD

CASTLE FOREGATE GOODS

SHROPSHIRE UNION YARD
SHREWSBURY (GENERAL)
ABBEY FOREGATE GOODS

LNWR/GWR
Upton Magna
WELLINGTON ►

POTTERIES JUNCTION YARD

LLANYMYNECH
PS & NWR

COLEHAM GOODS
Sutton Bridge Junction
SHELF SIDINGS

SHREWSBURY ABBEY
COLEHAM SHEDS

Hanwood Road

LNWR/GWR
Red Hill

WELSHPOOL
Hanwood
Cruckmeole Junction

LNWR/GWR

GWR

Berrington

MINSTERLEY

Condover
HEREFORD

HARTLEBURY

Potteries, Shrewsbury & North Wales Railway lines in Shrewsbury c1880.

◄ SHREWSBURY GENERAL
LNWR/GWR JOINT

ABBEY STATION

ABBEY FOREGATE

POTTERIES JUNCTION GOODS YARD
Signal Box

Sparrow Lane

Mill Race
Bell Lane
Lane

N

WELLINGTON ►

Engine Shed

Rea Brook

Midland Railway Carriage & Waggon Works

Carriage Shed

Coleham Junction

LLANYMYNECH
Signal Box

the appointment by the Receiver of one of the company's guards, a Mr Reeves, to control a skeleton staff to keep the more important assets of the company in reasonable order, the line and its fittings gradually decayed under the undergrowth that colonised the abandoned trackbed.

While the desolation continued so did the legal wrangles and there were several attempts to resuscitate the line. The company was officially wound up on 21 August 1882 and a Liquidator was appointed on 7 July. Selling an abandoned railway proved no easy task and it was not until 1888 that a new company was formed to try and re-open it. The Shropshire Railways was led by a Sir Richard Dansey-Price Green and attracted local support for plans to re-open the railway to Llanymynech and to complete the link to the Potteries — this time by a much more sensible route. The plans were passed on 7 August 1888 and on 25 August the remaining movable assets of the old company were auctioned in a sale that started at the Wellington Junction end of the line and visited each station along the route. Most of the rolling stock had simply been left where it was standing at the time of closure, except for the locomotives which were specially looked after in the locomotive shed at Shrewsbury. Most of the stock consisted of a variety of mineral wagons that went from just £3.10s each to £7. Potential purchasers had to agree to remove their bargains within six days, and the only rail access left was that running through the Midland Railway-Carriage & Wagon Works near the Abbey station up to the Coleham locomotive depots. Other legal and financial delays meant that the new company could not get possession of the line until the late summer of 1890 and work did not start on its restoration until 19 September. The Engineer was a J. Russell.

The extension to Stoke would have crossed the Wellington line by an overbridge before heading across the Severn near Pimley Manor and on to Hodnet on the Great Western's Wellington-Nantwich line, running parallel to that line to reach Market Drayton from where running powers over the North Staffordshire enabled the company to obtain access to Stoke itself. The company's Act stipulated that the Potteries' junction with the Wellington line had to be re-opened and the goods depot nearby rebuilt. The Contractor was Charles Chambers, who estimated the cost of relaying the existing line at £64,000, and work progressed quite steadily until 15 July the following year. By that time most of the track

Above left:
'Western' class diesel-hydraulic No D1033 *Western Trooper* backs on to the 8.55am Birkenhead-Paddington, as 'Modified Hall' No 6995 *Benthall Hall* on station pilot duties sits at platform 2. *R. Stephen*

Left:
Changing times at Sutton Bridge, Shrewsbury, as Class 47 diesel D1719 heads a West-to-North express past ex-LMS '2MT' 2-6-0 No 46525 shunting goods in the Shelf Sidings. *A. W. Martin*

Above:
A depressing scene on 23 January 1968 as a rake of condemned steam engines pause in the Shelf Sidings on their way to the breakers' yards of South Wales. *Shropshire Libraries*

Right:
A surprised train-spotter 'cops' an 'A4' Pacific, No 60010 *Dominion of Canada*, at Shrewsbury on 4 April 1967. The Class 47 hauling it is thankfully out of camera shot! *Shropshire Libraries*

had been relaid and the earthworks made good, but little had been done to the stations. The cause of the abrupt halt in the work in July was financial, with the Contractor claiming he had not been paid; there were writs and counter-writs from both sides but the Shropshire Railways had little money left with which to fight these legal battles and by 11 November the Receiver was called in. Despite new Acts authorising time extensions for the work and the issue of a new prospectus for potential shareholders in 1895, work was never restarted. There was a brief period of excitement following a feasibility study carried out in 1904 which recommended re-opening the line using a pair of steam railcars for passenger traffic that would just stop at track-side halts wherever there were potential passengers, but this would have relied on obtaining running powers into the General station from Red Hill. The Joint companies at the General station had already turned down an earlier request by the company in 1890 and

were little changed in outlook since then. The track and fittings decayed yet again, but in the summer of 1906 the directors were in correspondence with Holman F. Stephens, then running the East Kent Railway; he visited the line on 20 December and the end result of this visit was the formation of the Shropshire & Montgomeryshire Light Railway under Stephens' control, which got the necessary Light Railway Order on 11 February 1909. The '& Montgomeryshire' was added to acknowledge the financial assistance of Montgomeryshire County Council, which along with Shropshire County Council and several parish councils loaned money to the new undertaking. The Shropshire & Montgomeryshire never owned the line but leased it from the Shropshire Railways company which remained a separate company until Nationalisation.

Above:
Changing times: GWR 'Atbara' class 4-4-0 No 3397 *Cape Town* pilots a Dean 4-2-2 Single on a North-to-West express at Sutton Bridge and passes a Ramsbottom 0-6-0ST shunting out of the Coleham goods depot in the 1900s.
Ian Allan Library

Although the Shropshire Railways had relaid the track it had not creosoted the new sleepers and these were already rotten; Stephens had to replaced them with 36,000 new ones, but retained the original Potteries, Shrewsbury & North Wales track even though it was half a century old. The Bell Lane cutting section was not relaid and it seems the track from here was used elsewhere along the line where new crossing loops and sidings were needed, and the pointwork from the Potteries Junction yard was probably used in the new Exchange Sidings built at Meole Brace between the Shropshire & Montgomeryshire and the Joint companies' line to Welshpool. Bell Lane cutting was finally sold to the local council in 1937, and the section north of the Abbey Foregate road bridge was filled in 1960; the southern parapet of this bridge has somehow survived and the lower section of the earthworks now serves as a footpath over the Rea Brook. By the spring of 1911 the main line was ready, and on 11 April a train of ex-Midland Railway carriages was hauled from the Abbey terminus to Llanymynech by an ex-London & South Western six-coupled 'Ilfracombe' goods engine renamed *Hesperus*. Unlike the previous openings of the line this was done with a great deal of celebration and excitement. Rather embarrassingly, two days later *Hesperus* and her train were derailed on the sharp curve at Red Hill and had to be rescued by the London & North Western's breakdown crane; fortunately there were no

serious injuries. The Meole Brace Exchange Sidings were opened on 6 June and the Criggion branch soon after; the company settled down to enjoy a few years of relative prosperity.

By the 1880s the General station was becoming increasingly cramped for the vastly increased passenger traffic and was radically rebuilt between 1899 and 1902. Shortly afterwards it was to see a railway disaster that shook the country. The 1.20am Mail left Crewe a few minutes late on the morning of 15 October 1907, but the driver had made up some time by Whitchurch. However, the signalman on duty in Crewe Bank box on the approach to Shrewsbury saw it hurtle past at well over 60mph, far too fast to be able to slow in time for the 10mph restriction at Crewe Junction just outside the station, a few hundred yards away. He saw no sign of panic on the footplate and despite contradictory evidence later there seems to have been no whistle from the locomotive and no attempt to brake before the junction. The inevitable derailment caused mayhem, with carriages piling on top of each other, their flimsy wooden bodies breaking up like balsawood. In this

shambles 12 passengers, two guards, three Post Office sorters and both the engine crew died, with 31 others badly injured. The cause of the accident has never been explained satisfactorily; all the track had been relaid with the latest Great Western rails when the station was rebuilt. The carriages were all fairly new or had been overhauled within the previous year; the locomotive was one of the new 4-6-0 'Experiment' class, No 2052 *Stephenson*, built at Crewe and had only entered service the preceding January. In fact the engine had just been overhauled at Crewe a few days before the accident. The only cause of the accident seems to be that the driver had 'dropped off' briefly (he had been working for four out of the preceding five nights) and the fireman was too busy preparing for the station stop to notice him. Despite suffering extensive

damage to her frames and axles, and having her tender written off, *Stephenson* was repaired and put back into service.

World War 1 had no dramatic effect on Shrewsbury apart from the increase in coal trains heading northwards from South Wales to the Scottish bases of the Grand Fleet. At first these 'Jellicoe Specials' all ran through Shrewsbury but some were later diverted to relieve the burden on the Hereford line in particular. The war did of course lead directly to the Groupings of 1923. The Shropshire Union was at last amalgamated into the London & North Western in 1922 as a prelude to the forthcoming changes. The Shropshire & Montgomeryshire was left out of the re-organisations; the rest of the lines continued to be Joint, with the Great Western staying much the same as before, and the

Above:
Class 47 No 47.087 shunts a ballast train at Coleham; while in the PWM depot Class 08 shunter No 08.703 prepares to depart Hookagate, in April 1983. *Author*

London & North Western becoming part of the new London, Midland & Scottish company. Apart from the later introduction of 'foreign' engines from other constituent parts of the London, Midland & Scottish, little really changed until 1932 when the General station and the lines south were put under the operational control of the Great Western, though the London, Midland & Scottish continued to use the station and the lines just as before.

The Shropshire & Montgomeryshire company had inherited a line that served a very sparse population indeed, with few villages on the route. Stations were often at a distance from the villages they purported to serve which made matters worse, and the growth of road competition from the 1920s onwards placed the company in a difficult position. Despite opening new halts, reducing staff to a minimum, and cutting fares and costs the line was in deep trouble by the early 1930s and finally closed to regular passenger traffic, for the third time in its history, on 6 November 1933. Only the mineral traffic from Criggion and a daily goods train kept the line open until World War 2.

Along with most of the British railway companies, the Shropshire & Montgomeryshire was taken over by the Government and put under the control of the Railway Executive. The Executive did little to change things at first, and agreed to the company's plans to close the Kinnerley-Meole Brace section of the line in May 1940; this was cancelled by order of the Army which planned to build ammunition dumps along the line. The Army officially took over on 1 June 1941 although much of the rebuilding work had already been done and new exchange sidings had been built at Hookgate. The Army was to re-lay most of the track and build miles of new sidings to serve its depots. Its arrival on the old 'Potts' was not without incident, and the soldiers managed to live up to the line's reputation with several mishaps and embarrassing accidents, including blocking the Abbey Foregate road with two railway trucks after some over-zealous shunting at the Abbey station on Friday 13 March 1942 had pushed them over the buffer stops. After the war the Royal Engineers' Shropshire & Montgomeryshire Light Railway Detachment, No 1 Group carried on the line's operation until its closure. The line was transferred from WD (Military) to WD (Civilian) in 1947, manned by civilians. The Army was not the only operator to have the occasional mishap in the war years. In the space of a few days in May 1943 a London, Midland & Scottish tender engine ran away at Coleham, smashed through buffer stops and ended up in the Rea Brook nearly 40ft below, and a Great Western engine demolished the wall of one of the Mess Rooms at the other end of Coleham, injuring four people.

After Nationalisation, Shrewsbury was again in joint hands, with the new British Railways Western Region taking over the former Great Western lines, and the London Midland Region taking over those of the London, Midland & Scottish. There were a few changes, including the transfer of the Central

WD 'Austerity' 0-6-0ST No 193 pauses on Shrawardine bridge over the River Severn with an SLS 'Farewell Special' on 20 March 1960.
Hugh Ballantyne

Wales line from Craven Arms to the Western Region. The Shropshire & Montgomeryshire was officially a joint WD/British Railways (Western Region) line, except for the branch to Criggion that had never been taken over by the Army and went directly to the Western Region. The first casualty of the new era was the branch to Minsterley which was closed to passengers on 5 February 1951 remaining open to serve a large dairy at its terminus. Cruckmeole Junction was closed in July 1954, after which the crossing loop at Hanwood was the official junction, with the double line as far as Cruckmeole being operated as two single lines for Minsterley and Welshpool trains respectively. Goods traffic stopped running to Minsterley in February 1965, and by 1974 the Welshpool line was single from Sutton Bridge Junction onwards. Towards the end of the 1950s the Army began closing down its ammunition dumps and in late 1959 announced the closure of the 'Potts'. British Railways considered keeping the line open for

goods traffic but estimated only £269 a year in receipts, as against £8,716 in running costs. The line closed early in the following year with the last scheduled train running on 26 February 1960 followed by two 'Farewell Specials' organised by the Stephenson Locomotive Society in March. On 1 April the line was handed over to the Western Region for dismantling which began in earnest the following year. The Abbey station remained open for goods and oil traffic, and a short spur was built from the Severn Valley line to the Abbey line to maintain its rail access to the main lines.

The late 1950s had seen the beginnings of radical changes in the local railway scene, with the closing of many intermediate stations and the introduction of the new diesel multiple-units. In 1958 the Hereford line was rationalised with the new units and simultaneous station closures, followed by the Crewe line; in 1960 the same fate befell the Welshpool line, resulting in there being no intermediate stations between that town and Shrewsbury. Stations were also closed on the Chester line, but steam running continued for a few years, making the then non-stop portion between Gobowen and Shrewsbury one of the last 'mile-a-minute' steam routes on British Railways. The early 1960s saw a continuing decline in the town's railway fortunes; the

Above:
Steam returns to Shrewsbury. *King George V* **has been a regular visitor since its inaugural return in 1972. Here the locomotive makes a fine spectacle at Coleham in 1985.** *Author*

Severn Valley line closed to passengers on 7 September 1963, and through trains to Stafford had stopped by 7 September the following year after the Wellington-Stafford line was closed. From the start of 1963 Shrewsbury had been placed entirely under London Midland Region control, along with all former Western Region lines north of Craven Arms, coming under the Chester Division. By 12 February 1966 the area was under the enlarged Stoke District, where it has been ever since.

The most far-reaching changes followed the Beeching Report: the former London & North Western Railway main line to the Northwest was to be electrified, and the Great Western's Paddington-Birkenhead route was demoted from main line status. For a while the traffic passing through Shrewsbury increased as trains were diverted from the lines affected by the construction of the electrification programme, but by 1967 the first stage of the work had been finished. On 4 March the last through trains on the Great Western main line stopped; there were the usual enthusiasts' Specials to mark the event, but from that weekend all trains heading east from Shrewsbury stopped at Wolverhampton High Level, with just one through train to London a day — to Euston. Coleham locomotive depot was closed at the same time and Shrewsbury looked like being just an unimportant railway crossroads served by a handful of diesel multiple-units.

However, despite constant threats of yet more closures and the scare of the Serpell Report of 1983 (one part of which would have left the town with no railways at all), Shrewsbury is actually enjoying a tentative revival in its services, thanks largely to progressive local management and enterprising schemes such as the 'London Saver' tickets. The through services to London (Euston) are again up to a respectable level, and through trains are beginning to be extended northwards to Chester as well. With radical resignalling and other new plans for the area served by Shrewsbury in the pipeline, it would appear that the town's role as a railway centre, albeit not as important as it once was, is fairly secure. This new confidence since the mid-1960s is exemplified by the recent restoration of the General station and the move of the local offices to the refurbished buildings from the ugly offices in Chester Street, opened in 1960 by the Western Region.

2 The Development of Passenger Services

Shrewsbury & Chester Railway

The Shrewsbury & Chester Railway began taking passengers from Shrewsbury before its line to the town was actually opened, arranging for stage coaches to connect with trains on the Ruabon-Chester portion of its North Wales Mineral section that had opened in November 1846. Once the first trains through to Shrewsbury started in 1848 the first timetable consisted of six trains in each direction on weekdays, reduced to three on Sundays. As was usual at the time, third class passengers were only taken by a few trains, although they at least had the benefit of 'covered carriages on all trains'. One morning and one evening train carried all classes, and from Shrewsbury these were the ridiculously timed 3.35am and the more reasonable 6.15pm. Other trains left in between at 7.15am, 9.25am, 11.25am and 3.15pm. In the opposite direction the morning train left Chester at 3.50am, with others at 8.00am, 10.40am, 1.40pm, 5.15pm and 8.15pm, the last carrying third class passengers. The fastest trains took one hour 45 minutes. On Sundays just one train in each direction took all classes, the 7.05am from Shrewsbury and the 3.50am from Chester, with other trains from Shrewsbury at 2.18pm and 6.20pm and from Chester at 9.10am and 8.15pm; the Sunday trains were slower than those on weekdays, the fastest taking two hours 10 minutes.

By the beginning of 1854 the early morning trains had been dropped and there were seven trains each way with some working through Shrewsbury and on to Wolverhampton. The Sunday service had been reduced to just two trains each way, plus one through train from Chester that went to Wolverhampton. There was also an unusual train on the days when the Shrewsbury Cattle and Cheese Fairs were held; a second class carriage was attached to

Below:
An unidentified 'John Hick' class 2-2-2-2, one of the many Webb three-cylinder Compounds quickly demoted to local passenger work, seen here at the site of Potteries Junction on a Shrewsbury-Stafford local in the 1900s.
Real Photos

the 6.00am coal train from Ruabon, calling at Gobowen and Baschurch. Most trains were timed to connect with the short Shrewsbury & Chester branch line from the main line at Gobowen to Oswestry.

The Shropshire Union: Shrewsbury to Stafford

The Shropshire Union opened with three trains in each direction to and from Stafford. Only the 6.00am from Shrewsbury carried third class passengers, with the other trains leaving at 12.10pm and the 5.00pm; the average journey time was one hour 35 minutes. In the opposite direction the 8.30am carried third class passengers, but the 2.15pm and 8.45pm trains did not. There were two trains in each direction on Sundays, and again only one of these carried third class travellers. By the summer of 1850 the service had been improved to four trains a day in each direction, but still only one taking all classes. All the Shropshire Union trains were timed to connect with the London & North Western main line trains to Euston at Stafford, and by the mid-1850s there were the first through carriages from Shrewsbury to London (Euston). The first through trains followed shortly afterwards, timed to leave Shrewsbury at 10.20am, 1.00pm and 5.00pm, arriving at Euston at 3.45pm, 7.30pm and 9.30pm; naturally these only carried first and second class passengers. By this time there were four other local trains on the Stafford route in each direction. From Euston

the three through trains left at 6.30am, 10.00am and 12 noon, arriving at 1.15pm, 3.30pm and 7.25pm. There were three trains in each direction on Sundays, but none of these went through to Euston. Until 1861 the Shropshire Union could truthfully claim to be 'The only route between London and Shrewsbury without break of gauge or change of carriage'. Just what carriages the company used for their London services is difficult to find out, but those for local trains seem to have been handed down from other lines. During the Shrewsbury Show in June 1850 the number of people using Shrewsbury trains was enormous; the Shrewsbury & Birmingham borrowed some carriages from the Shropshire Union to add to one of its trains, but one of these was the cause of a derailment. In the subsequent examination of the incident it was found that all the carriages were in a shocking condition, and 'that the decayed state of the wood . . .' is in such an unsound state as to have rendered them unfit to be used for the conveyance of passengers'.

Shrewsbury & Birmingham Railway

In contrast to those of the Shropshire Union the carriages on the Shrewsbury & Birmingham were considered very good at the time:

Below:
A pair of Webb 'Experiment' class locomotives double-heading a Hereford local out of Shrewsbury station in the 1900s. *Real Photos*

they were built and maintained by private contractors. The first class carriages were described as 'exceedingly roomy and fitted up luxuriously'; second class were 'ample in width and height, many of them also having cushioned seats', while 'even the Third class carriages are closed and have glass windows'. Until the line was opened through the tunnel at Oakengates, there were four trains to and from Oakengates station from Shrewsbury, with just the first and last trains, the 6.45am and 6.45pm from Shrewsbury and the 8.45am and 8.15am from Oakengates, carrying all classes. Other trains left Shrewsbury at 9.35pm and 4.15pm, and Oakengates at 2.15pm and 5.15pm. There were two trains in each direction on Sundays, one of which carried third class passengers. The journey time was 40min. By November 1849 the service was extended to the High Level station in Wolverhampton, but passengers wishing to continue into Birmingham had to find their own way to the Grand Junction line station in order to do so while the London & North Western held up the opening of the Stour Valley line. The Stour Valley was finally opened on 1 July 1852 but the London & North Western intially timed its trains running on it to make connections with the Shrewsbury line as inconvenient as possible. By this time there were seven trains each way between Shrewsbury and Wolverhampton; the average wait at that station for Stour Valley trains was 20min, and the fastest

time from Shrewsbury to Birmingham (New Street) was 2hr 10min. Once the Shrewsbury & Birmingham began to run into New Street on 4 February 1854 the journey time was immediately cut by 10min. Then, in November, the trains began running into the Low Level station at Wolverhampton and on over the mixed gauge lines of the Great Western into Snow Hill. Until the opening of the Great Western line north of Birmingham, passengers travelling to and from the Shrewsbury lines from the Great Western had been taken by omnibus, free of charge, between Snow Hill and New Street stations. The Great Western increased the number of trains between Birmingham (Snow Hill) and Shrewsbury to nine in each direction, with the fastest then taking just 1hr 25min. For some time after the move from the High Level to Low Level stations, there was a strange service still running from the High Level station consisting of a carriage leaving there in time to be added to the Shrewsbury bound services from the Low Level station at the junction where the new route left the old. This lasted until the end of February 1859 and was not worked in the other direction.

Shrewsbury & Hereford Railway

Until the line was extended southwards to Hereford, there were four trains to and from Ludlow. By 1853 these were timed at 9.20am, 1.00pm, 4.00pm and 7.00pm from Shrewsbury and arrived in Ludlow at 10.45am, 2.20pm, 5.10pm and 8.20pm. In the opposite direction trains left Ludlow at 7.40am, 1.15pm, 4.30pm and 6.15pm, arriving at Shrewsbury at 9.00am, 12.20pm, 5.40pm and 7.36pm. The 1.00pm from Shrewsbury and the 1.15pm from Ludlow

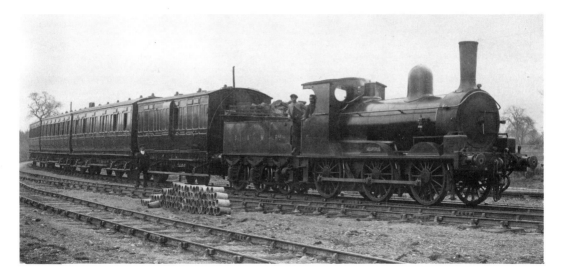

had coach connections with Hereford. In addition to these trains first and second class carriages could on request be added to the 5.00am goods train from Shrewsbury and the 8.15am goods from Ludlow, and there were extra trains on Tuesdays for the Shrewsbury markets.

By the start of the 1860s there were seven trains in each direction running through to Hereford, and after the lease of the line the Great Western and London & North Western ran their own separate trains before reaching joint running agreements in the spring of 1864 after which the only train not run jointly was the Mail, which was in the hands of the London & North Western. In 1866 there were still seven trains in each direction with the fastest taking 1hr 40min. In addition there was one train that just went to and from Ludlow, and some market day trains. Extra carriages were added to trains at Church Stretton on Shrewsbury market days, and at Craven Arms

on Ludlow market days. One unusual feature of the 10.25am train from Shrewsbury was that it had a slip coach for Church Stretton, only stopping at Craven Arms before reaching Ludlow. There were two trains in each direction on Sundays, one being the Mail. For some reason the up Mail to Shrewsbury was run jointly.

Shrewsbury & Crewe

The Shrewsbury & Crewe line opened with five trains in each direction, the fastest being the 5.20pm from Crewe which arrived in Shrewsbury at 6.30pm. In the opposite direction the fastest was the 7.40pm from Shrewsbury which arrived at Crewe at 8.50pm. The 9.25am from Shrewsbury carried third class carriages, as did the 6.00am and 7.40am trains from Crewe. On Sundays there was just one train in each direction, leaving Shrewsbury at 3.00pm and Crewe at 11.30am. The first class fare was 5s 7d, third class 2s 8d. By 1866 there were seven trains a day, but still only two carrying third class passengers, and still only one on Sundays. The fastest time was now just 55min on trains stopping only at Whitchurch and Nantwich on the way. One early complaint by passengers was the use of broken-up Grinshill sandstone as ballast; this tended to powder and got into the carriages and people's clothes. The Shrewsbury-Crewe trains were often timed to connect with those on the Shrewsbury-Hereford line, and later with those running to Welshpool.

Shrewsbury & Welshpool, and the Minsterley Branch

The Minsterley branch was always worked as a branch line from Shrewsbury, and no trains terminated at Hanwood (the nearest station on the main line to Cruckmeole Junction). The service changed little over the years. In 1866

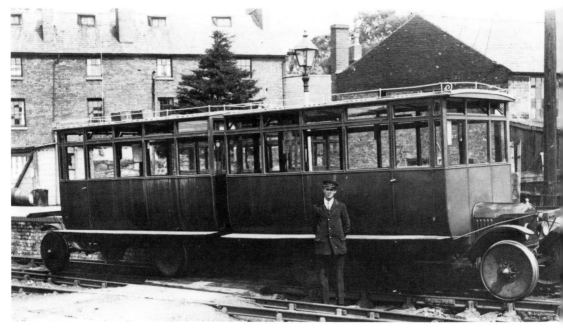

there were four trains in each direction, the first of the day from Shrewsbury being a mixed train departing at 6.45am. The first train from Minsterley also carried goods as well and left at 7.00am. The journey time varied between 30 and 40min.

By 1866 there were six trains in each direction between Shrewsbury and Welshpool; these had been worked by the London & North Western up until 1865 when they were worked jointly by them and the Great Western. All trains, except the 1.45pm and 2.50pm departures from Shrewsbury, and the 4.00pm and 8.40pm departures from Welshpool, took first, second and third class passengers. At first there had been no Sunday trains, but in 1866 there were two in each direction, one of which was the Mail. The fastest train was the 4.00pm from Welshpool, which took just 48min.

Severn Valley Railway

There were just four trains a day running over the Severn Valley line between Worcester and Shrewsbury after it opened, a situation unchanged in the first few years of its existence. Just one train ran on Sundays in each direction. The West Midland Railway, which initially ran the line, had ambitions to create a new trunk route from Worcester to London, rivalling those main lines of the Great Western and London & North Western from the capital to the Midlands. These fancies never really materialised, and although Severn Valley trains theoretically connected with trains for London, the journey took several hours longer than the route by way of Stafford or Wolverhampton. In any case all thoughts of rival routes were quashed after the company was amalgamated with the Great Western.

Most trains stopped at all stations and none were particularly fast. In 1878 a branch was built from Kidderminster on the Oxford, Worcester & Wolverhampton's (later West Midland Railway) former main line to Bewdley on the Severn Valley line, with the result that some trains were diverted to Kidderminster instead of Worcester. At about the same time more of the former through trains to Worcester began terminating at Hartlebury instead, and there were some that connected with a Bewdley-Hartlebury shuttle service.

Potteries, Shrewsbury & North Wales Railway

When the 'Potts' opened so optimistically in the summer of 1866 this company ran five trains in each direction between Shrewsbury and Llanymynech, where connections were made with the Cambrian Railways' line between Oswestry and Newtown. Although the company had running powers through to Oswestry, these were seldom, if ever, taken advantage of. The average time of the trip was 50min for the 20 miles, so that the 25mph speed limit imposed in later years by the Board of trade could have had little effect! There were two trains on Sundays, and all trains took third class passengers. By the autumn one of the weekday trains had been dropped, and by 21 December so had all the rest. After the reopening two years later several of the trains carried on from Llanymynech up the Nant-mawr Quarries branch as far as a station optimistically called Llanyblodwell, although the village of that name was some distance away. Some of the stations became conditional stops as an economy measure, but by the mid-1870s the train services were beginning to

LMS 4-6-2 'Duchess' Pacific No 6226 *Duchess of Norfolk* with a Plymouth-Manchester and Liverpool express at Hadnall, north of Shrewsbury. Its streamlined casing is already getting the worse for wear by 26 July 1941.
Peter Clay/LoS

stop bearing much resemblance to the official timetables as lack of maintenance and the increasing use of mixed trains took its toll. This rather alarming decline in the company's fortunes is illustrated in an incident at Coleham Junction in 1875. On 28 December the 4.40 ex-Llanymynech arrived at the junction running late, as usual. It consisted of two passenger coaches, three cattle trucks and one of the company's few remaining brake-vans, and was hauled by one of the 0-6-0 tanks. The cattle trucks had to be attached to the next Great Western goods train heading east, so the engine and cattle trucks were detached and set off up the Bell Lane cutting to the Potteries Junction yard; the carriages were left standing on the single track by the disused signalbox. There was no proper guard on the train, as that particular gentlemen had taken sick and the company had no reliefs available. Instead the stationmaster from the Abbey station was acting as guard, but by the time he had set off to warn on-coming trains one of the mineral trains from Nantmawr went past him and ran into the carriages. No one was seriously injured in the collision, fortunately, but the matter did come to the attention of the Board of Trade which warned the company about its safety standards. In 1875 the 'Potts' abolished second class fares in a bid to create more custom, but really it was not the lack of

passengers that killed the line, more the pressing burden of creditors.

Fares, Excursions and Specials
It is of course very difficult to compare 1980s prices with those of the mid-19th century. In 1849 the first class fare to London (Euston) was £1 15s, with second class a mere £1: no doubt both of these were more than the average weekly wages of the time. Even a third class single to Stafford would cost 2/5d. The cheapest fares were those of the excursions, and probably most of the people who went by these never used the railway at other times. Many of these outings were organised by local businessmen, in most ways the fore-runners of today's travel agents. In the Whit Holidays of 1849 it was possible to go to Chester and back for 3/6d, and to the Isle of Man and back for just 9s. The most popular destination for excursion was the North Wales coast, with trains running to the popular resorts along the Chester & Holyhead line. Excursions to

Above:
This Webb 2-4-2T was still in charge of Minsterley branch trains in 1942 — No 6691 heads for Shrewsbury past Hookagate on 24 March. The bridge in the background carries the Shropshire & Montgomeryshire over the main line to Welshpool. *Peter Clay/LoS*

Aberystwyth were also very popular, and it was actually the Potteries, Shrewsbury & North Wales company which provided the best value and most convenient timings for these shortly after their opening. Their excursions went by way of the Cambrian Railways from Llanymynech, but after that first summer of 1866 the company does not seem to have done much about starting them up again and it was left to the other railways. Other special trips were run to the bigger towns such as Liverpool, Manchester and Birmingham — and there were also very early versions of the present day London Saver tickets.

One unusual passenger service was started in the summer of 1853, before the railways through to Welshpool and Newtown had been built. The Shropshire Union owned the canal link from what is now called the Llangollen Canal at Welsh Frankton, through the Montgomeryshire Canal to Newtown. At Rednal the canal crosses under the Shrewsbury & Chester line near to Rednal station. A fly-boat service

was started, of 'Swift Passenger Boats' to connect with the trains and take passengers to Welshpool and Newtown. It was introduced along with a similar but shorter service from Llangollen Road station to Llangollen, but neither appears to have been economically viable, and they were soon stopped.

One other category of special trains included those taking people to the various Shrewsbury Shows, and the Shrewsbury Races; both of these events were very popular, and there were a great many trains from all over the country and surrounding areas to them, so much so that the station couldn't always cope with the traffic.

Development of the London Traffic and the Great Western Main Line

By the beginning of 1855 the Great Western had started running fast trains on its new Shrewsbury lines into Birmingham and thus competed with the London & North Western for the Shrewsbury-London traffic. Three trains ran into Birmingham designed to connect with the Broad Gauge trains from there to Paddington. They left Shrewsbury at 6.30am, 10.25am and 5.50pm and after a change at Snow Hill, Birmingham, passengers could be in Paddington by 11.25am, 3.05pm and 10.30pm, travelling by way of Oxford. All trains carried third class passengers. The

Right:
'Castle' class 4-6-0 No 5078 *Beaufort* on a Liverpool-Plymouth express approaching Sutton Bridge on 27 June 1942.
Peter Clay/LoS

4hr 30min timings of the two faster runs compared reasonably with the usual London & North Western timings by way of Stafford. To go to Euston in the London & North Western's new third class-carrying slow train took seven hours, so at least the Great Western attracted many third class passengers on to its new service.

On 1 May 1857 certain Great Western trains running between Birmingham and Chester by way of Shrewsbury were extended northwards over the Birkenhead Railway to Birkenhead by an agreement with that company; this was a prelude to the Great Western's joint lease of the line with the London & North Western and gave it a trunk route between the Midlands and the Mersey. On 1 October 1861 a narrow gauge through service was started that went from Birkenhead to the newly-converted Paddington by way of Shrewsbury, and the Great Western could compete on a fairer footing with the London & North Western for the Shrewsbury-London traffic. Three trains ran in each direction, and by 1866 these had settled down to become the 10.05am, 10.45am and 1.40pm from Shrewsbury arriving at Paddington at 6.50pm, 3.50pm and 6.50pm. The unusually slow time of the 10.05am was due to its being a slow stopping train; in the reverse direction trains left Paddington at 8.00am, 10.00am and 12 noon, arriving in Shrewsbury at 12.40pm, 2.37pm, and 5.18pm. Despite no longer having to change at Birmingham there was no improvement in the time taken, and in fact the Great Western

didn't really seem to care much about its main line to the north past Wolverhampton.

In 1880 the Great Western surprised everyone by introducing new and faster trains, completely changing the timetable. The star of these new services began running in June of that year, leaving Paddington at 4.40pm and arriving in Shrewsbury at 8.37pm before carrying on to Birkenhead. The most dramatic improvements in its timings were north of Wolverhampton, and the 3hr 50min to Shrewsbury lopped nearly an hour off the previous fastest train. In the other direction the fastest train left at 1.18pm (having left Birkenhead at 11.45am) and, only stopping at Wolverhampton, Birmingham, Leamington Spa and Oxford, arrived in Paddington at 5.25pm — just slightly slower than the down train. Because of the wars in South Africa at the time this service was nicknamed the 'Zulu', sometimes referred to as the 'Northern Zulu' to distinguish it from a Broad Gauge express of the same name. The arrival of the 'Zulu' meant that there were now four through trains daily between Birkenhead and London via Shrewsbury and two on Sundays. The 'Zulu's' schedule was changed fairly often in the next few years with some stops added and some taken off; at one stage in 1888 the portion north from Shrewsbury to Birkenhead was non-stop, apart from detaching a coach for Chester just outside that town. By the end of the century the 'Zulu' was still the fastest of the Northern Division's expresses and left Paddington at 4.55pm, reaching Shrewsbury at

8.33pm, just 3hr 38min later. In the up direction it left Shrewsbury at 1.33pm and arrived at Paddington at 5.20pm, stopping only at Wolverhampton, Birmingham (Snow Hill) and Leamington Spa, with slip carriages for Oxford and Reading. There was a Luncheon Car attached to each train.

In 1892 the line had the first express to be equipped with proper corridor carriages, designed by Dean. The set consisted of four 50ft coaches built on the old style short bogies: there was a first, second and third-class coach with a brake third and usually a van. The carriages were lit by oil-gas, were steam-heated and had separate ladies' and gentlemen's toilets. The inter-connecting corridors were offset to the side, which caused problems when one or other of the carriages

had to be taken out for repair, and also with marshalling carriages the 'right-way' round; the doors of these connecting corridors were kept locked, the guard having the key. They first ran on revenue-earning service on the 1.30pm Paddington-Shrewsbury-Birkenhead service on 7 March.

In the early summer of 1910 the Bicester cut-off was completed and considerably reduced the distance to London (by nearly 20 miles) and the time taken to get there. Before the cut-off was opened the fastest time from Paddington was just over 3½ hours, whereas by 1912 the fastest train reached Shrewsbury in just under three hours.

The London & North Western still ran through carriages from Shrewsbury to London (Euston) right up until Grouping. In fact in

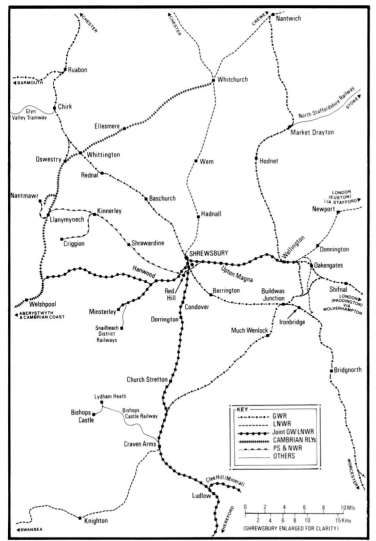

Left:
Railway routes to Shrewsbury.

1880 it was possible — by using through trains, through carriages or changing just once — to get from Shrewsbury to London by no less than 16 trains: seven were London & North Western, six Great Western via Birmingham, and three Great Western ones by Worcester and the Severn Valley, although this last route took seven hours. In that year the London & North Western still kept the through carriages on the train leaving Shrewsbury at 10.20am although these now got into Euston at 3.00pm, an improvement of 15min on the late 1850s. The other two trains ran at 12.45pm and 10.08pm, with the carriages reaching Euston at 5.30pm and 4.30am; the 10.08pm was the Mail train. In the reverse direction there were only two trains with through carriages, the 5.15am arriving in Shrewsbury at 9.53am, and the 9.15pm (Mail) arriving at 3.00am. There were several semi-fast trains to Stafford for connections with the London & North Western's main line. On Sundays there was just one train with through carriages from

Shrewsbury, the 10.08 arriving at Euston at 5.30pm; in the other direction there were through carriages on the 10.09am (arrive Shrewsbury 3.35pm) and the 9.00pm (arrive Shrewsbury 3am) trains from Euston. Once the Bicester cut-off had been opened the Great Western route was both shorter and quicker.

The timings to the north on the Great Western main line had also been reduced with the introduction of the faster expresses. Several trains from Shrewsbury in the 1890s terminated not at Wolverhampton or Birmingham, but at Leamington Spa, from where some also started. The reason for this unusual service probably lay in the fact that Leamington had become the southern limit of the Northern Division. The number of local trains on the lines from Wolverhampton to Shrewsbury and Shrewsbury to Chester had increased in number during this time but were not that much faster. One new aspect of the main-line trains was the introduction of through trains to the south coast by way of the London & South Western and South Eastern railways. Between July 1863 and October 1869 there had been through carriages from Birkenhead through Shrewsbury and down the main line to Reading, and from there to Dover and to Hastings. By the turn of the century new services had been introduced, including through carriages from Dover and Folkestone through Shrewsbury to Birkenhead, the

Below:
Hawksworth 4-6-0 'County' class engines began to appear on passenger workings north of Wolverhampton in the early 1950s. Here the first of the class, *County of Middlesex*, approaches Shrewsbury station with a Paddington-Birkenhead express.
Russel Mulford/Michael Embrey

Left:
0-6-0PT No 3725 with a local train for the Severn Valley slows to collect the single line token at Sutton Bridge.
Russel Mulford/ Michael Embrey

Below left:
Ex-GWR 'Manor' 4-6-0 No 7818 *Granville Manor* comes off the Welshpool line with a passenger train from the coast in 1958.
Russel Mulford/ Michael Embrey

Bournemouth express via Reading, and the original 'Shakespeare Express' which actually ran between Bristol and Birkenhead via Stratford-upon-Avon, Birmingham (Snow Hill) and Shrewsbury.

Rails to Wales

In the latter part of the 19th century the Welsh coast resorts were becoming increasingly popular. Both the Great Western and the London & North Western were more than a little interested in the development of this traffic and had the advantage of sharing the Shrewsbury-Welshpool line to the Cambrian Railways route to the coast. As early as the 1870s the London & North Western had started running through carriages on the Cambrian lines to Aberystwyth. They met the Cambrian Railway at Whitchurch as well as at Buttington Junction, but this advantage over the Great Western was more than countered by the latter's own route from Ruabon to Dolgelly, and through coaches were put on this line and main line trains used to connect with the trains running on it.

The passengers travelling from London or from the industrial Midlands usually had to pass through Shrewsbury by way of the Great Western via Wolverhampton, or the London & North Western via Stafford. Both companies made use of the Abbey Curve to avoid Shrewsbury station, especially on excursion trains but by the turn of the century on regular turns as well. In 1904 the two companies were running trains in direct competition with each other. The 9.30am from Paddington ran non-stop from Wellington to Welshpool using the Abbey Curve and its through carriages arrived at Aberystwyth on the same train as those of the London & North Western that had also left London (Euston) at 9.30am. The London & North Western working was a summer only one. These carriages arrived in Aberystwyth at 5.20pm. There was an 11am working from Euston with through carriages, arriving at Shrewsbury at 2.45pm and at Aberystwyth at 8.45pm; the Great Western didn't have a second fast working, only one that left 20 minutes after its first train, and that arrived in Aberystwyth at 7.40pm after the carriages had been left waiting at

Shrewsbury for nearly half an hour. There was a third set of through carriages from Euston at 1.30pm, arriving in Shrewsbury at 6.10pm and in Aberystwyth at 9.35pm. In the opposite direction both companies' through carriages left on the 9.10am train from Aberystwyth with the London & North Western carriages beating their rivals to London by just five minutes; with the through carriages on the 1.00pm from Aberystwyth the situation was reversed. The London & North Western had a third set of through carriages leaving at 2.45pm, reaching Shrewsbury at 5.47pm, and Euston at 11pm. The Great Western also ran shorter through carriage routes between Birmingham and Aberystwyth and also to other resorts further along the coast, all of which stopped at Shrewsbury.

The Central Wales route had a fairly quiet existence for many years after it was finished. The leisurely trains between Shrewsbury and Swansea were infrequent and took around five hours to complete the journey. In 1880 trains left Shrewsbury at 6.45am, 10.30am, 2.10pm and 5.55pm, arriving in Swansea at 12 noon, 3.25pm, 6.40pm and 10.45pm. In the opposite direction trains left Swansea (Victoria) at 6.15am, 9.55am, 12.30pm and 4.20pm, arriving in Shrewsbury at 11.15am, 2.20pm, 5.25pm and 9.47pm. There was also one train from Shrewsbury that terminated at Knighton, and two for Shrewsbury that started from there. In the 1890s and early 1900s the spas at Llandrindod Wells, Builth Wells, Llangammarch Wells and Llanwrtyd Wells became fashionable resorts for the upper middle classes and the train services on the Central Wales line were drastically improved to cope with the additional traffic. The London & North Western began a series of through carriages for the Central Wales line, detached from main line expresses at Stafford and run with Shrewsbury or Aberystwyth trains to Shrewsbury before being attached to trains for Swansea. The 1.30pm from Shrewsbury took only four hours to reach Swansea. Other through carriages from other areas were sometimes attached to the Central Wales trains, including ones from Leeds and Manchester. In 1910 there were still only five through trains from Shrewsbury to Swansea, but there were in addition two trains terminating at Builth Road, and one each terminating at Knighton and Llandrindod Wells. The 5.10pm semi-fast from Shrewsbury arrived in Swansea (Victoria) at 9.05pm, just under four hours later. There were also five through trains in the other direction as well as some locals, and the 8.00am from Swansea was the fastest train on the line, taking just 3hr 28min to cover the 115 miles to Shrewsbury; however, its

Below:
'Castle' class 4-6-0 No 5079 *Lysander* heads a North-to-West express south of Shrewsbury on 2 March 1957. *H. A. Chalkley*

timing could be affected by several conditional pick-up only stops on the way.

The North-to-West Expresses

In the early days of railway development in the area the Great Western and the London & North Western both desperately wanted to get from Shrewsbury through to South Wales to benefit from the coal traffic from that area, and both had managed to do so. The passenger traffic was not considered to be too important and was not really developed that much. Then, in 1886, the Severn Tunnel was opened and the Great Western realised the possibility of taking some of the traffic from Bristol and the southwest away from the Midland Railway, which had up to then monopolised any of this traffic going to the north and northwest by

means of its Bristol-Birmingham route. Together with the London & North Western the Great Western started an experimental express service between Bristol and Crewe, by way of the Severn Tunnel and Shrewsbury; trains were worked by the Great Western south of Shrewsbury, and by the London & North Western north of the town. The new service began on 1 July 1888 and was an immediate success; it was the Great Western's first main cross-country route. Originally there were three trains in each direction, with a fourth added the following summer. At Crewe, Pontypool Road and Bristol various through carriages were added to the trains going, as Ahrons puts it, 'from everywhere to everywhere else'. Through carriages came from all over Britain, with some from Manchester, Glasgow, Edinburgh and Leeds attached at Crewe, and others from South Wales attached

Left:
Ex-LMS Pacific No 46235 *City of Birmingham* heads a West-to-North express up out of Shrewsbury. Note the smokebox — a legacy from the streamlined casing with which it was originally built. *H. A. Chalkley*

Below:
Talyllyn Railway Preservation Society specials could be relied on to produce a wide variety of motive power. A goods 2-8-0, No 4701, heads a Paddington-Towyn excursion towards Shrewsbury on 24 September 1960. *M. Mensing*

Above:

A Welshpool-Birmingham train, hauled by No 7802 *Bradley Manor*, **uses the Abbey Curve to avoid Shrewsbury station on 22 July 1950.** *W. A. Camwell*

Left:

Hughes 2-6-0 'Crab' No 42859 on a Paignton-Manchester train waits at Shrewsbury station, with Stanier 'Black Five' No 45031 heading a local for Chester, on 24 August 1963. *Ian G. Holt*

Below left:

Standard Class 4 4-6-0 No 75004, with double chimney, takes the Welshpool line with a Paddington-Pwllheli train on 4 July 1964. *A. W. Martin*

at Pontypool Road. After the conversion to standard gauge of the lines past Exeter, through carriages started to run to and from Plymouth and the resorts of Devon, attached and detached at Bristol. These through carriages and the through carriages on other trains running all over the country must have made Shrewsbury a somewhat confusing place to catch a train from.

Much of the North-to-West work was done at night. The first train of the day from Bristol in 1910 was the 12.25am arriving in Shrewsbury at 3.30am and Crewe at 4.20am. This was followed by the 9.00am which had through carriages from Bristol to Glasgow and was called the 'Scotch Express'; this arrived in Shrewsbury at 11.55am and Crewe at 12.38pm. Next was the 9.30am from Bristol which got into Shrewsbury at 12.30am and Crewe at 1.30am, followed by the 12.45pm from Bristol that had a Luncheon Car and reached Shrewsbury at 3.45pm, and had through carriages for Liverpool, sent on after arrival at Crewe at 4.25pm. The 2.20pm from Bristol arrived in Shrewsbury at 5.23pm and Crewe at 6.17pm. The 4.10pm from Bristol boasted a Luncheon, Tea and Dining Car and arrived in Shrewsbury at 7.13pm and Crewe at 8.02pm, having through carriages from Plymouth to Liverpool. The last train of the day was the 7.40pm from Bristol arriving in Shrewsbury at 10.40pm and Crewe at 11.35pm. As well as having through carriages from Bristol to Glasgow it picked up through carriages from Cardiff to Newcastle at Pontypool Road. The service in the opposite direction was pretty much the same, and there was one other train to note, the 'Cardiff Express' which ran non-stop on the Shrewsbury-Hereford portion taking only just over the hour to do it in; it left Shrewsbury at 2.35am and Cardiff could be reached by through carriages at 5.43am.

By 1938 the service was, if anything, even more complicated with a profusion of through carriages. Through carriages ran from Penzance to Liverpool, Manchester and Glasgow; from Liverpool and Manchester to Cardiff; from Manchester to Paignton, Kingswear, Newquay and Penzance; from Birkenhead to Plymouth; from Liverpool to Swansea (Victoria); from Blackpool (North) to Cardiff and Swansea (Victoria); from Glasgow to Plymouth; and even from Colne to Truro. Many of these workings were obviously summer services only. The number of through carriages on this route remained very high for much of the 1930s and trains would often be composed of 17 of them, very well loaded especially in summer. Several of the trains were no longer

stopping at Crewe or Bristol and what had previously been just portions of longer trains were now trains in their own right, such as the Manchester-Cardiff and Manchester-Plymouth services.

Express timings were continued on the North-to-West route after nationalisation and by the early 1960s were often diesel-hauled, initially by Western Region diesel-hydraulics, but later by London Midland Region Class 47s. The route managed to keep at least some of its services after the radical changes in the mid-1960s, but following the announcement of the summer timetables in 1970 the route was demoted to a secondary cross-country line and the service was shortened to run between Cardiff and Crewe and run by three-car cross-country DMU sets equipped with buffet facilities. The buffet was not well used and was soon dropped. For a brief time in 1976 InterCity DMU sets were used, but these were replaced by locomotive-hauled stock. Class 25s took over much of the workings but at the start of the 1980s Class 33s displaced from the Southern Region arrived. In 1984 two trains travelling north from Shrewsbury were again extended to Manchester, the faster of the two being the 9.58am (7.45am ex-Cardiff) which arrives in Manchester at 11.28pm. This compares favourably with prewar timings; the fastest train between the two places in 1938 had been the 4.00am which ran non-stop to Manchester (being the Plymouth-Manchester express) arriving at London Road at 5.40am. There are possibly plans to extend more of the present Cardiff-Crewe trains to Manchester (Piccadilly) in the future; not all the trains on the route are locomotive hauled as the stopping trains are all worked by DMUs. At present there are (1984-85) six Cardiff-Crewe trains and seven in the other direction;

The Shropshire & Montgomeryshire Light Railway

For the reopening in 1911 of the 'Potts', Stephens bought two second-hand rakes of carriages, one ex-London & South Western and one ex-Midland Railway — the latter coaches were used for the inaugural service out of the Abbey station. Originally there were three trains in each direction between Shrewsbury and Llanymynech with just one on Sundays. By 1912 a fourth train had been added from the Llanymynech direction only, as well as a second Sunday train, but as a wartime economy the Sunday services were suspended in October 1916 and were never reinstated. In 1923 there were four trains in each direction, one of which terminated at Kinnerley. All

Above left:
Brush Type 4 D1718 heads a Swansea-Manchester train into Shrewsbury on 12 June 1964. *Derek Cross*

Above right:
Brush Type 4 D1733 (in blue) at Shrewsbury station with a Manchester-Plymouth express on 4 August 1964. *Ian Allan Library*

trains took an hour, and sometimes more, to reach Llanymynech and were on average 15min slower than the services of the Potteries, Shrewsbury & North Wales trains. This was partly due to the 25mph speed limit imposed on all light railways and mainly due to the use of mixed trains which led to interminable shunting manoeuvres at each station along the line. Apart from the inevitable road competition one of the things that finally drove away the few passengers there were was the introduction in the late 1920s of the infamous railcars. Known locally as the 'Rattlers', they more than lived up to their name. At least the slow steam-hauled trains had some degree of comfort; the railcars had none. A passenger could even travel in luxury if he desired, paying a supplement on occasions to use the pride of the railway's ancient carriage fleet, an 1848 (or possibly earlier — as an 1844 lithograph shows an identical carriage being used for a royal traveller) former Royal Saloon off the London & South Western Railway that was tragically scrapped after World War 2. The railcars, whatever their economical virtues, could never have been described as comfortable. They had wooden seats and were literally made up of two bus bodies back-to-back on rail wheels, driven by the petrol engine of either of the buses depending on which way the train was going (unlike a modern DMU). Two sets were bought, one based on a Ford Model 'T' type bus, the other on a Wolseley-Siddeley pair. They were incredibly noisy, thanks to their hollow wheels and cheap construction, and could be heard miles away. Introduced in the mid-1920s, they did not last long and both had

been withdrawn by 1931. They were not at all popular with the drivers, one of whom was sacked after crashing a set in 1930; he was probably relieved to depart!

Just before the end of the passenger services on the line there were still four trains in each direction, but all stations between Llanymynech and Shrewsbury, with the exception of Kinnerley, Ford & Crossgates, Nesscliff & Pentre and Meole Brace, were conditional stops. The fastest trains officially took 50min. In 1933, despite all the economies and new halts the line finally ceased to take passengers with the exception of special excursions, usually on Bank Holidays. Sometimes a carriage would be added to one of the mineral trains, but after *Gazelle* had been restored she and her trailer would be used for such workings, often starting from Meole Brace rather than the Abbey station. During World War 2 there were passenger trains for the troops run to the Army's timetables, and liberty trains would work to the Abbey station at weekends, usually by 11.00pm. There was still the occasional passenger excursion until the end of the line in 1960.

Local Services
Most of the local services changed little over the years after the latter part of the 19th century and provided a reasonably good train service to and from Shrewsbury. The number of trains and the timing of trains changed little, but the carriages got more comfortable. By 1880 there were still four trains in each direction on the Minsterley line at about the same time of day as when the line opened, though the times of the trains were all down to

Above:

A typical Severn Valley train towards the end of the line's existence: an Ivatt 2-6-2T has just hauled two carriages and a van into No 2 bay in the first week of September 1963, just before the line was closed. *Andrew Muckley*

about 30min, and by now there were no mixed trains involved. Little had changed by the end of the century but by 1938 there were actually six trains a day with three extras on Saturdays and most train times were down to 25min; the situation had changed little when the line closed to passengers in 1951.

In 1880 the Severn Valley line had had five trains from Shrewsbury, either to Kidderminster or Hartlebury, and four trains to the town, with the occasional train through to Worcester. By the turn of the century there were five trains running into Shrewsbury, two starting at Worcester, and the other three at Hartlebury. From Shrewsbury there were two trains through to Worcester, two to Hartlebury and one to Kidderminster. There was also a train to and from Bridgnorth. By 1938 there were still five trains a day to and from Shrewsbury, and since the start of the 1930s there had been a Sunday train service. This now consisted of one train to and from Bridgnorth, and one round trip from Birmingham (Snow Hill) nicknamed the 'Fishermans Special'; this train left Snow Hill at 7.22am and reached Shrewsbury by way of Kidderminster at 10.30am. On the return trip it left at 8.00pm, arriving at Snow Hill at 10.47pm. Soon after World War 2 the service was again reduced to four trains each way and Sunday services were stopped. Great Western diesel railcars were introduced on the line, some working from Shrewsbury on occasions but most working south of Bridgnorth. The service was more or less kept the same until closure, although extra trains did make an appearance and Sunday services were re-introduced. The line began to have diesel multiple-units for a brief period just before it closed.

The local services to Welshpool in 1910 consisted of five trains in each direction taking roughly 45min to cover the distance and stopping at all stations. There were two trains in each direction on Sundays. By 1938 there were six trains each way but the Sunday trains had been dropped and this service was more or less maintained until the line was 'rationalised' in 1960. Effectively this means that all the stations between Shrewsbury and Welshpool were closed, and after the cessation of steam running in 1967 all trains were DMUs. Since 1965 all trains from Shrewsbury had run through to the coast following the closure of the former Cambrian services north of Buttington Junction to Whitchurch. Apart from the odd excursion and a summer Saturday only through train from Euston, there are no locomotive-hauled trains on the line, but there are plans to change this.

There were seven trains in each direction running between Shrewsbury and Hereford in 1880 and most stopping trains took nearly 2hr 30min for the trip. In addition there was one train to and from Ludlow. Apart from the Mail train to Cardiff and back there was only one train on Sunday, a Parliamentary stopper. By 1910 the stoppers ran in between the North-to-West expresses. There were three semi-fast trains and four stopping trains Shrewsbury and Hereford, as well as three stopping trains just to Ludlow, the slowest train taking 2hr 13min. In the other direction the service was not quite the same, with only one stopping train running through from Hereford; there were five semi-fast trains, with two morning trains starting from Ludlow. Passengers from the smaller stations had to change at Craven Arms unless they caught the 7.30am stopper from Hereford. There were two

Left:
A few days later the last trains ran on the Severn Valley — a DMU bound for Hartlebury waits in No 1 bay at Shrewsbury station on 7 September. *Russel Mulford/Michael Embrey*

Below left:
After local steam-hauled passenger trains had officially stopped, 'Jubilee' 4-6-0 No 45593 *Kolhapur* leaves Shrewsbury for Crewe on 8 April 1967. *John R. P. Hunt*

ping trains between the two places. There were around five of these each day in the 1880s, taking about an hour to complete the journey. By 1910 there were five trains in each direction; several trains were semi-fast as far as Wellington before stopping at all stations from there to Stafford. In addition there were five stopping trains between Shrewsbury and Wellington over the joint lines each way. On Sundays there was just one stopping train through to Stafford, with three to Wellington; in the other direction there was the one stopping train from Stafford, but only two from Wellington. By 1933 the number of stopping trains had increased dramatically, with 12 trains from Stafford and nine from Shrewsbury. This was due mostly to the demise of the faster trains connecting with London trains at Stafford, as the London traffic was by now firmly in the hands of the Great Western. By 1937 there were 12 in each direction, and just one fast train running through. The average journey time was still just under the hour. Shortly before the line closed there were six stopping trains and one fast train in each direction, with no through trains on Sundays; a change had to be made at Wellington.

One of the more unusual local trains on the Shrewsbury-Crewe route in 1880 was the Sunday train that went between the two towns via Stafford, taking 3hr 5min for a trip that usually took half that time. By the 1900s there were five stopping trains in each direction, as well as a few semi-fasts and the expresses. By the 1930s there were eight in each direction, plus one train from Shrewsbury that terminated at Whitchurch. Local services took about 1hr 30min to get to Crewe. The service remained fairly similar until 1958 when diesel multiple-units were introduced in June in connection with those on the Shrewsbury-Hereford line. In 1961 seven trains from Crewe were stopping at most of the remaining stations (and this line didn't actually suffer that much from station losses) and there were nine in the opposite direction; these were fitted

trains in each direction on Sundays, besides the express running each way. By 1938 there were seven stopping trains of one kind or another between Shrewsbury and Hereford as well as two locals that terminated at Ludlow; the Sunday service had been increased to three a day, one stopping train and two semi-fasts, one in each direction. The situation had only changed slightly in 1957, when there were six trains one way and eight the other. From June the following year the local services on the line were altered radically with the closure of many stations and the introduction of diesel multiple-units which cut the journey times substantially. The only intermediate stations to survive were at Church Stretton, Craven Arms, Ludlow and Leominster, all of which are now unmanned. With the North-to-West's demotion in 1970 the local and Cardiff-Crewe services were combined.

Shrewsbury-Stafford trains were of two types, the fast trains connecting with the London expresses at Stafford, and the stop-in with the North-to-West expresses, most of which stopped at Whitchurch only. On Sundays there were three stopping trains from Crewe and five from Shrewsbury. After 1970 the trains were run as part of the Crewe-Cardiff services.

The Central Wales line was to become an unimportant secondary route in the 1920s after the Spa towns had ceased to be so fashionable. Nevertheless, it was still a vital link for people living in the isolated areas through which it ran. There were 12 trains from Shrewsbury in the late 1930s, and there were still through carriages from London (Euston)-Swansea on the 2.40pm from Shrewsbury (arriving in Swansea at 6.59pm) and from Manchester and Liverpool to Swansea and Pembroke Dock on two others. There was also a Saturdays only working between York and Swansea. The average times of the stopping trains was about 4hr 30min but the times did vary considerably. The line was under threat in the Beeching Report, and has been under threat ever since although services have survived. Diesel multiple-units now work the line which has been reclassified as a light railway since 1972. After the closure of Swansea (Victoria) in 1964 trains terminated for a time at Llanelli, but now run into the former Great Western station in the town. There has been extensive advertising to attract customers to the line, and there are at present five trains in each direction with no Sunday trains; the fastest journey time is now around 4hr.

The line between Wolverhampton and Chester, the old combined route of the 'Fighting Shrewsburies', enjoyed a good local service right up until the 1960s. In 1938 there were 10 trains from Shrewsbury on the Chester line; some were semi-fast to Gobowen, and others called at all stations. These had to be timed to fit between the Paddington-Birkenhead expresses. There was a similar service in the opposite direction, together with some market day only trains. Several of these local trains carried on to Birkenhead. Following the closure of intermediate stations the Gobowen-Shrewsbury timings were down to almost a mile-a-minute and were the fastest passenger steam timings left on the railways. The services from Wolverhampton-Shrewsbury were the last regular stopping passenger services to be hauled by steam on the London Midland Region. All the work, with the exception of the through trains from London (Euston), is now done by DMUs introduced on the Chester line in 1960 and on the Wolverhampton line in the mid-1960s. After the end of the Paddington-Birkenhead trains in 1967 the trains to Wolverhampton and beyond were again running into the High Level station as they had done over a century before.

Below:
Class 47 No 1700 hauls one of the few locomotive-hauled trains from the Cambrian coast on 25 August 1973 — this is the Summer Saturday Aberystwyth-Euston train near Upton Magna. *C. Plant*

Above:
Class 33 No 33.002 heads towards Shrewsbury with a Cardiff-Crewe train in January 1985.
Author

Below:
This three-car DMU for Wolverhampton is passing the site of Potteries Junction in January 1985. *Author*

Class 47 No 47.442 heads a Shrewsbury-Euston train over Belvidere Bridge in April 1983. *Author*

The Demise of the Great Western Main Line

After the Grouping the Great Western maintained its fast services north of Wolverhampton and its route was by then the quickest between Shrewsbury and London. In the 1920s there were some very fast runs north of Birmingham and for a while some of these were run non-stop between Snow Hill and Shrewsbury. Some never stopped even at Shrewsbury — but these were special Aintree Grand National trains with which the Great Western tried to take some of the race-going traffic off the London, Midland & Scottish. In 1924 the company introduced its systemised train departures from Paddington, with all trains for Birmingham and the north leaving at 10min past the hour. The services north of Shrewsbury were never really speeded up from its 1910 timings; trains to the town did become slightly faster, but not by that much.

The star turn of the main line only went as far as Shrewsbury on it. This was the 'Cambrian Coast Express', which had originally been one of the trains of through carriages to Aberystwyth. By 1921 it had become a train in its own right, leaving Paddington at 9.50am with portions for both Aberystwyth and Pwllheli; complete with Restaurant Car it did not officially become known as the 'Cambrian Coast Express' until 1927, leaving at the new systematic time of 10.10am. For many years the train used the Abbey Curve at Shrewsbury and avoided the

station altogether. It was a Friday and Saturday working only up until World War 2, and although the train continued in one form or another it did not become officially the 'Cambrian Coast Express' again until 1951, working summer Saturdays only. By 1954 it had become a daily train in the summer and was speeded up considerably; a restaurant car was taken as far as Shrewsbury. In the 1960s its time was moved on to 12.10pm from Paddington. It was finally stopped in 1967. In September 1954 a sleeper service was started from Shrewsbury, leaving at 10.15pm at first, later changed to 11.10pm arriving in Paddington at 5.10am. The down sleeper left at 12.05am arriving in Shrewsbury 5.16am. Shrewsbury briefly had one other named express in the 1960s — the 'Pines Express' that ran initially between Manchester and Bournemouth and was re-routed many times; in 1963 the Nantwich to Wellington line was closed, and the 'Pines', which had been running on that line briefly from Crewe, was re-routed through Shrewsbury.

Prior to the completion of electrification of the Euston lines, the old Great Western route through Shrewsbury saw a brief acceleration of its timings and an increase in its services

together with the use of modern diesel-hydraulics. All this ceased in March 1967, when the electrification work had been finished. Prior to that there had been 11 through trains to London (Paddington) and 17 trains in total went to Wolverhampton (Low Level). Afterwards there was just one train in each direction to London (Euston), with theoretically 17 others connecting with Euston trains at Wolverhampton High Level. There were for a short period still two daily trains into the Low Level station as well. From the latter part of the 1970s these through services to Euston were slowly and steadily improved to the extent that there were (1984-85) five through trains from Shrewsbury and four in the other direction, as well as one Saturdays only working from Euston. Train times are down to 2hr 50min. There are three trains from Shrewsbury to Euston on Sundays, with two in the return direction. In 1984 one train in each direction was extended to Chester and there

Above:

No 37.255 on a Special at Shrewsbury in January 1985. *Author*

are plans to do so with more trains later. Ordinary local services to Chester have changed little, and there have been no services through to Birkenhead since 1967.

The new timetables introduced in May 1985 brought about the promised improvements in the InterCity services to London. There are now seven through trains from Shrewsbury to Euston, with six in the return direction; there is a through train roughly every two hours, taking well under three hours to complete the trip. In addition there are three through trains on Sundays. The present London service is at last back to the same standard as prevailed before the changes of 1967.

In connection with these trains, a second through train from Euston to Aberystwyth

Above:
One of the more unusual DMU workings is a daily through train from Chester to Aberystwyth, which waits at Shrewsbury's Platform 7 on 27 March 1985. The bridge on the right carries Howard Street over the former rail access to the Shropshire Union yard, which was bricked up in August 1985. *Author*

now runs on summer Saturdays and there are other plans to improve the Cambrian coast route. Already two trains in each direction run to the coastal resorts from Crewe via Shrewsbury, with a third added on summer Saturdays.

More improvements have been made to the old North-to-West route. Buffet services are again available between Newport and Shrewsbury on most of the locomotive hauled services, but the most exciting innovation has been the introduction of the first 'named' train

to run through Shrewsbury since the demise of the 'Cambrian Coast Express'. The new 'Welshman' runs between Holyhead and Cardiff, running via Crewe and Shrewsbury. There is one train in each direction, with an extra train between just Bangor and Cardiff. Quite how long this new service will last is uncertain, but it does reinforce Shrewsbury's role as the main railway junction linking all parts of the Principality.

One other type of passenger service should be mentioned in passing. Throughout the summer months, and especially at weekends, several special excursions pass through Shrewsbury from various parts of the country en route for the Welsh resorts, on mystery tours or more interestingly on preservation specials steam-hauled from Newport through to Chester.

With the current modernisation plans it would seem that Shrewsbury's passenger traffic is at least safe for the time being.

3 Stations and Signalling

The Shrewsbury & Chester Railway had been authorised to build a station at the corner of Cross Street and Chester Street; the Joint line from Wellington had permission to terminate at two points in the town — the Howard Street Canal Basin and near the English Bridge on Abbey Foregate. The Chester company along with the Shropshire Union and the Shrewsbury & Birmingham, and the temporarily postponed Shrewsbury & Hereford Railway, quickly saw that it was in everyone's mutual interest to build a joint station. A Joint Station Committee was formed which met for the first time in April 1847 to plan such a station and a site was chosen between the Castle and the County Gaol.

The Committee received tenders for the necessary work ranging from £23,933 1s 8d to as high as £42,768, and accepted an intermediate one by Thomas Brassey of £30,963 11s 2d. The total cost of buying the land, raising the earthworks and building was about £100,000. The track layout and signalling was designed by Stephenson and Robertson and the station building itself was designed by Thomas K. Penson, an architect from Oswestry who also designed the stations on rest of the Shrewsbury & Chester line. The resulting structure was and, despite a great deal of rebuilding and alterations still is, a very fine piece of architecture.

Built in Grinshill stone at a cost of £6,000 its style has variously been described as Tudor-Gothic and Neo-Jacobean, and is probably somewhere between the two. It was designed to complement the nearby 16th and 17th century buildings of the old Shrewsbury School, which like the station itself have recently been restored and are used as the Central Library. Originally there were just two storeys with a symmetrically placed central clock tower some 70ft high. The clock was an eight-day one with a 12ft pendulum built by the famous clockmakers Joyce & Co, Whitchurch, and was installed in 1850. The tower also boasts a fine oriel window.

The main entrance was originally under the oriel window but was later moved to the west side of the tower; there was another entrance nearer to Castle Foregate as well. Each of the large windows has heavy transoms and mullions and each piece of their architrave was decorated at the ends with a label head of several basic types; these do not seem to have any particular significance, any more than the heraldic designs on most of the building do. The building was finished off with fine ornamental chimneys, a richly-decorated embattled parapet and a roof topped off by intricate metalwork. The ground floor contained the booking offices, waiting rooms and refreshment rooms (the latter being run by outside contractors), and the upper floor contained the station offices, committee rooms and traffic offices. There was also a well-equipped kitchen in the cellar. By 1854 the building had been extended westwards in the same style to abut on to the Castle Foregate road, and this extension effectively had an extra floor as the basement had windows out on to the street.

There were two main passenger platforms, each 16ft wide. Nearest to the main buildings was the departure platform, 650ft long;

Below:
An early photograph of the General station, probably dating from the 1870s.
Shropshire Libraries

Above:
Cross Street Bridge in the 1890s. The original brick-arch bridge was first widened when the line from Crewe was built. The small structure on the left is a rather elaborate urinal!
Shropshire Libraries

Right:
Beginning work on the widening of the Severn viaduct c1899, looking towards the station.
Shropshire Libraries

From the south the approach had to be made on a bridge over the river high enough not to interfere with the barges plying to and from the Shrewsbury quays. Baker designed a brick viaduct of seven arches each of roughly 45ft span, carrying three lines of track 36ft above the average level of the river. Work started on this bridge in early 1849 and it was ready shortly before the line to the east was opened. From the north the tracks had to cross both Cross Street and the Castle Foregate just before the station itself. The former was spanned by a brick arch, the latter by a

opposite was the arrivals platform, 450ft long. Most of the platform areas were covered by a wrought iron roof 'with an immense glass sky-light' and a 70ft overall span supported on pillars at each side. There was no passenger footbridge at first, but the Dana footpath crossed over the tracks by a timber bow and string twin-span bridge 190ft long on its way between the Castle walls and the river. To comply with the old laws of rights of way this had to be roped off once a year — usually on Good Friday — but the laws have long since changed.

The approaches to each end of the station by rail were difficult to construct. On the one side was the river and on the other the main road to the north. The station site had to be raised considerably above the level of the ground, involving the moving of 50,000 tons of earth.

single-span wrought iron arch made by the Brymbo company in which Henry Robertson had a large stake. It was of 64ft span and carried four lines of track.

William Patchett was appointed Station Superintendent just before the station first opened and remained so for the better part of half a century. Contemporary guides describe the station of 'The United Companies' as being 'commodious, and provided with ample and well conducted refreshment rooms', and state that 'the politeness and civility of the officers connected with this station is proverbial'. As these quotes come from contemporary guides for the Shrewsbury & Hereford and Shrewsbury & Chester Railways, perhaps their objectivity is questionable. Certainly the station had its fair share of problems, the most costly of which was the acute shortage of water,

despite being close to the river. Before an efficient pumping house had finally been built, water was actually carried from springs near Hencott in wooden pipes to the station over a mile distant. Letters quoted in the Station Committee minutes complain of over-charging in the refreshment rooms, no heating in the waiting rooms and of lost parcels. There was a 40s fine for anyone caught smoking on the station premises or for anyone found to be drunk. The rules for the staff were much stricter, and included fines for lost goods and incivility.

A Mr Parry was appointed Chief Booking Clerk at £200 per annum. All the station staff had to be smartly dressed, and no one over the age of 40 was employed by the Station Committee. The minutes report that many of the staff were tempted away to similar but better paid jobs elsewhere; the work of this Committee is summed up by the outcome of a meeting in March 1850 which saw a Constable and a Head Porter reprimanded for 'soliciting Christmas boxes', the Carriage Inspector suspended for being drunk on duty, the go-ahead for building new urinals, and the refusal of a rise in Pointsmen's pay. In 1855 the Booking Clerk disappeared with £59 of the station's receipts. The station had all the usual carriage and wagon turntables, and shunting

Top:
Castle Foregate in February 1985, looking south.
Author

Centre:
Detail of the architrave and label heads at the General station in 1985. *Author*

Bottom:
The station tower, etched in snow in February 1985. *Author*

Above:
Shrewsbury did not have a Station Hotel as such, but all the better hotels in the town sent coaches to meet trains. The Raven Hotel's coach enters the forecourt in the early 1900s.
Shropshire Libraries

within the station areas was by shunting horses stabled in Howard Street. At first these were provided by outside contractors but the station acquired its own shunting horses in 1858.

The opening of the line to Crewe in 1858 meant there were some changes needed at the northern end of the station, including the widening of the Cross Street bridge by means of a girder extension on the west side of it. With the imminent opening of the Severn Valley and Welshpool lines at the start of the 1860s the station was enlarged further between 1861-63 with the addition of a new platform near to Howard Street and the lengthening of both the original platforms by some 400ft; the arrivals platform became an island platform in the process. An extra roof span was also built to cover the extra platform space and the existing roof was lengthened by 250ft. The Dana footbridge was now converted into a footbridge for use by passengers with steps down to each platform. New sidings were also added, so that Shrewsbury actually had more sidings than Crewe did; the total cost of the extension was in the region of £45,000. At this time there were about 77 passenger trains in and out of the station each

day. In 1866 the station track was re-laid using steel rails, and as previously mentioned the opening of the Abbey Curve in the following year greatly improved the congestion in the station itself. The two older platforms were used mainly for main line trains, while the opened up face of the arrivals platform and the new platform at the Howard Street side were used for locals.

Unlike most important railway towns Shrewsbury has never had a purpose-built station hotel. The Station Hotel of today, a public house, was called the 'Grapes' until World War 2 and had no connection with the railway companies. The building of a station hotel was discussed by the companies on the Station Committee but nothing was done about it probably because the town already had a good number of quality hotels. The better hotels sent their carriages to the station yard to meet the more important main line trains. In 1878 a monumental fountain became a landmark in the forecourt, erected in the memory of William Clement, a local surgeon. Little more was done to the station until the 1890s, by which time it was once again becoming over-crowded and incapable of handling the ever-increasing traffic passing through. Various plans were put forward for its rebuilding. The widening of the Severn viaduct had been discussed as early as 1860 though this had been rejected on grounds of cost, but now the scheme was resurrected because of necessity. New girder bridges were to be built on either side of the older viaduct, and the work started

in 1899. Similar girder bridges were also built on either sides of the bridges over Cross Street and Castle Foregate. The station itself was to be rebuilt, but a radical plan to demolish the old buildings and start afresh was thankfully rejected. Between 1899 and 1902 the station platforms were altered to fit into the new scheme. The old departure platform was the only one that was kept intact, being extended over the new girder bridge across the river, and a double bay was built at its southern end. The total length of the elongated platform was nearly 1,000ft, each of the bays being 350ft long. The old departure platform was numbered 7 (south end) and 10 (north end), the bays being numbered 8 and 9. A huge new island platform replaced all the other platforms; it was extended across the river and was indented by a double-tracked bay nearly 450ft long at its southern end. The platform face opposite Nos 7 and 10 (ex-departure platform) was 1,014ft in length and was numbered 5 and 6; the two bays were numbered 3 and 4 with the remaining face of the island platform being numbered 1 and 2. Most of these platforms were used fairly indiscriminately by different trains for different directions, but Nos 1 and 2 and Nos 7 and 10 were used for most of the main line expresses.

A huge overall roof was built over the new platform extensions to the south of the Dana footbridge consisting of several transverse spans of glasswork on steel frames. The older roof was kept at the north end of the station

for the time being and at the south end a new footbridge of heavy opaque glass in a wooden frame was built. The expansion of the station had meant that many buildings had to be demolished, including some on the Castle Foregate and all on the south side of Howard Street. The old Butter Market, by then a warehouse on the opposite side of the street, was rebuilt slightly to fit in with the new alignment of Howard Street, which accounts for its slightly odd shape.

The most unusual aspect of the station enlargement was the additional floor given to the station buildings. This may not seem that uncommon, but most extra floors are built on to an existing building. At Shrewsbury, the floor was added underneath it. This delicate operation involved the extension and excavation of the cellars and digging out the old station forecourt to the depth of 12ft; the Clement Memorial was moved to the Quarry Park prior to work beginning. The additional floor was built in exactly the same style as the rest of the building and today it is difficult to imagine that the ground floor of the station is actually 50 years younger than the rest of it. The famous glass verandah running the length of the building dates from this period. The new entrance to the station was by way of a subway, which had access to the platforms by a central stairway to the new island platform and other stairs to the old departure platform. The new booking office was at the entrance to the subway. Hydraulic lifts were installed for handling parcels and gas lighting and heating was installed. The rebuilt refreshment rooms were now at the south end of Platform 7, on Platform 10, and in the new buildings erected on the new island platform, which is where the refreshment room and bar is at present. Wyman's Ltd had two book stalls, one on Platform 10 and the other near where the present booking office is, at the top of the stairs leading to the subway from the island platform.

A new road was built from Cross Street up to a new dock for carriages near the Crewe Junction end of the station, and there was also a dock for horse-drawn traffic at the Howard Street side of the station, replacing the earlier one nearby. In 1924 the old overall roof over the north end of the station was removed and replaced by individual platform canopies; the old supporting walls of the original roof can still be seen near the present No 7 Platform. Part of this roof had collapsed under the weight of snow in the winter of 1887 killing an unfortunate ex-town councillor who happened to be underneath at the time. When the station came under the Great Western's sole control in

1932 the porters ceased to be self-employed; they had up until that time, paid an annual rent of 6d per year. The staff of the Joint companies had built their own refreshment room in 1914 at the south end of the old Platform 9. An elected Committee ran it and staff could buy shares in it at 5s a share and a dividend was paid annually. Known to all and sundry as 'The Tavern' it was forced to move from its original site to a room off Platform 10, and it finally closed for good in 1968.

Apart from a few minor changes, the only major alteration until the 1960s was in the renumbering of the platforms in the new British Railways pattern of having No 1 as the nearest to the main station entrance. Platforms 9 and 8 became Platforms 1 and 2; Platforms 7 and 10 became the new Platform 3; Platforms 5 and 6 became the new Platform 4; the old Platform 4 became Platform 5; Platform 3 became Platform 6; and Platforms 1 and 2 became Platform 7. The renumbering was completed in 1950 and has remained the same since.

In 1961 the Western Region embarked on a new rebuilding of the station. The first stage involved removing the footbridge at the south end of the station which was always too inconvenient for passengers being so far away from the subway entrance; its main use was by railway enthusiasts, though its heavy glass

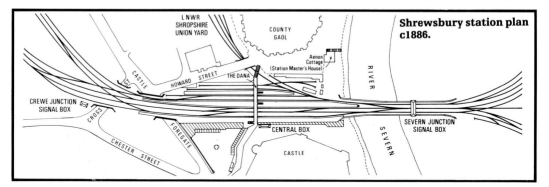

Shrewsbury station plan c1886.

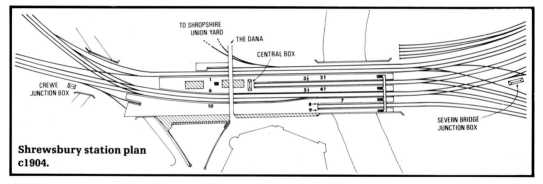

Shrewsbury station plan c1904.

Left:
An early, but undated, aerial shot of the station showing the northern part of the overall roof that was removed in 1924. The view was probably taken c1920. *Shropshire Libraries*

Below right:
GWR 'Saint' class No 2943 *Hampton Court* stands at the then Platform 10 (now No 3) on 15 July 1939. *Peter Clay/LoS*

Bottom:
The General station frontage in 1948.
Real Photos

Above right:

GWR 0-6-0 No 2516 stands in the island platform bays with a special in 1955. Note Central Cabin signalbox at the end of the bay, and the width of the roof, supported only at each side. *Lens of Sutton*

Right:

Ex-GWR '51XX' 2-6-2T on station pilot duties at Shrewsbury on 2 June 1952. *G. Raxter*

Below:

A brace of ex-LMS Pacifics at the north end of Shrewsbury station in the 1950s: Nos 46237 *City of Bristol* and 46251 *City of Nottingham*. *G. Sackville*

made it of little help for observations. A legacy of the 1899-1902 rebuilding was the 'dog-leg' on the main down platform, the old Platforms 7 and 10 (Platform 3 in the new renumbering). This was where the bridge section of the platforms began and the through lines were reduced from three to two between the down and island platforms. Just why this was never widened at the turn of the century is something of a mystery, but it was causing problems soon afterwards as the length of trains got longer and arrivals on the down platform from London or from the south would often have to leave carriages blocking the middle through line. Shrewsbury was never a station that was approached quickly and there always seemed to be a signal stop before the platforms could be reached. To alleviate the problem, the southern end of the new Platform 3 was dismantled and a slimmer platform of concrete trestle-build erected in its place. The adjacent bay lines also had to be re-aligned. The line from the old face of Platform 3 was then extended to create three running lines all through this side of the station, and a new cross-over was put in to carry London traffic on to this new extension.

At the same time there were other changes, including the removal of the old scissor crossing at the end of the island platform bays (Platforms 5 and 6) as these were now seldom used with the demise of steam hauled locals; engines no longer had to run round their trains in the bays. The turntable near the Sutton Bridge box was also removed along with the line running from the up side of the station and Howard Street Yard to it, and in its place a new engine line was put in on the other side of Sutton Bridge box, which was completely relocked at this time; the relocking took place over several Sundays and over 40 hand signalmen were needed whilst the box was out of action. The first colour signals also

Above:

Removing the original arches from the Castle Foregate Bridge in 1962, while in the background the Chester Street offices near completion.
Russel Mulford/Michael Embrey

appeared, two starters in the island platform bays and one on the approach off the Rea Viaduct.

By this time the overall roof at the south end of the station was in a very poor state of repair and parts of it had already been dismantled. By 1964 most of the roof had been removed and new shelters were built on the platforms affected. Temporary lights were put in before new ones were supplied. The roof had many of the old gas pipes carried in its girders so these were removed and the station was converted to electric lighting; at the same time the old single-spindle operated station clocks were replaced by electric ones and the old lifts were also converted to electric power.

After the removal of the British Railways offices to Chester Street the station buildings were left rather neglected. Apart from a few cosmetic changes like the building of a new

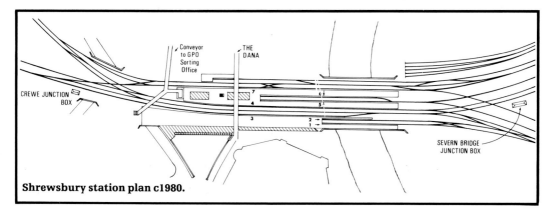

Shrewsbury station plan c1980.

booking office at the top of the central stairs to the subway and the opening of a travel centre at the entrance off the station forecourt, the overall picture was one of decay, matching the run-down of local railway services in general. All the refreshment rooms bar the one on the island platform were closed and the newsagents' stalls disappeared. The buildings were left to dry rot and finally in 1967 British Railways (London Midland Region) announced outline plans to demolish the old station buildings; naturally, there was a huge outcry from locals and conservationists alike and the plan was quickly dropped. By the 1970s British Railways seemed to take more interest in this architectural asset and the stone work was cleaned of decades of grime; then at the start of the 1980s it was happily announced that money had been found to restore the buildings,

along with the elegant bridge at Belvidere, and work started with gusto in 1984 with a completion date of mid-1985. After their short period in Chester Street, the district offices are to return to the refurbished station and a new power signalbox is due to be fitted in as well. Further plans include the rationalisation of the track plan at the south end of the station to get rid of many of the expensive to maintain points and diamond crossings, singling the Abbey Curve and lifting one of the through lines in the station itself. Platform 3, at present seldom used for nothing but football specials, will be re-instated as one of the main platforms. The restoration of the station shows just how a bit of imaginative planning can save our railway heritage and give a new and useful life to historic buildings.

To prevent delays and crowding at the station in the 19th century there were ticket platforms on each approach to it, used in particular by local stopping trains. The

Left:
The south end of the station shortly after the overall roof was removed, but before the new shelters were erected. The concrete trestle section of Platform 3 dates from the removal of the 'dog-leg' in 1961. A Western Region 'Warship' stands on Platform 4. *Lens of Sutton*

Below:
Nos 1 and 2 bays on 25 October 1966. BR Standard Class 4 No 75016 is alongside a Central Wales line DMU. *R. E. B. Siviter*

earliest recorded one was that near Underdale Road on the joint line to Wellington, which appears on a working timetable of 1866 as Abbey Foregate Platform; it was south of the line adjacent to the goods depot and six trains a day had to stop there for ticket inspection, three each of the Great Western and London & North Western Railways. At exactly what date it was changed to a 'drop' station is not known, but it was certainly advertised on public timetables 'for alighting only' in 1886. It was closed officially on 30 September 1912.

One of the other ticket platforms became a 'drop' station; this was on the Hereford line just north of the English Bridge Junction of the Abbey Curve where the main line approaches the station. The platform was reached by a footpath and steps from what is now the car-park of the Gay Meadow ground of Shrewsbury Town FC. Although it is not listed on the 1866 timetable it was certainly in existence in the mid-1870s and was converted to a 'drop' station around 1887. Called English Bridge Platform, it was closed on 2 May 1898.

Neither of the other two ticket platforms became 'drop' stations as neither had any reasonable access to a public road. The platform on the Crewe line was to the east of it, just north of Crewe Junction near the entrance to the Castle Foregate goods depots; it had disappeared by the end of the century. The other was on the Chester line near where it passes the Castle Foregate goods warehouse. Because of the cramped space it had to be built in between the two running lines, which was probably an unwitting cause of a fatal accident. On a winter evening in 1867 a young lady arrived at the station only just in time to catch the 5pm Chester train, but she had no

Top:
Class 33 No 33.001 heads south from Shrewsbury station with a Crewe-Cardiff train.
Brian Morrison

Above right:
A newly painted Class 37 heads the Crewe test train out of Shrewsbury past the redundant Castle Foregate goods yard on 25 March 1985.
Author

time to buy a ticket; the booking clerk gallantly let her get on the train while he made out the ticket and caught her up, by which time the train was moving out of the station. Jumping on to the running board of the carriage he gave the lady her ticket, but as he jumped off he misjudged where he was, fell on to the edge of the ticket platform, slipped under the train and was killed as the carriage wheels ran over him. The platform had gone by the late 1890s, probably removed in preparation for the rebuilding of the station. Shrewsbury General

Left:
Abbey station in use as a coalyard c1900.
L&GRP courtesy David & Charles

only became a closed station (admission by ticket only) in 1914.

Shrewsbury has for many years been noted for its special events — The Shrewsbury Show, the Flower Show, West Midlands Agricultural shows and so forth. At one time it also had a racecourse. To cater for the extra traffic generated by these events, extra passenger station accommodation had to be found. For the Races, temporary wooden platforms were built near Crowmere Road on the Wellington line; even the New Yard goods depot was used for racegoers on occasion. For other shows, the Coleham goods depot was often used for specials departing on lines to the south up until World War 2.

Before its amalgamation with the Shrewsbury & North Wales company the Shrewsbury & Potteries Junction Railway had planned a station at the point where its line crossed the Wellington line. The idea was for trains from the Stoke direction to run into a platform beside that main line before reversing and crossing it on the level in order to start descending the Bell Lane cutting towards Coleham Junction. The estimated cost was £170,000. A spokesman for the Joint Committee said 'I know of nothing so absurd in the Kingdom', and who can blame him? The idea was patently unworkable. Apart from the fact that the site was at that time in the middle of fields well away from the town centre, neither the Great Western nor the London & North Western could be expected to stop their trains at a point just over a mile from the General station and arrange their timings to connect with the Potteries' trains; the idea of shunting passenger trains across a very busy main line was obviously unrealistic. The modified proposal was just as naive. Trains arriving from each direction to the station on the Potteries' line would terminate on either side of the main line and passengers wishing to carry on would cross over by a footbridge. Both schemes were inevitably thrown out, and a new station substituted at the Abbey Foregate, opposite the magnificent Abbey church founded by Roger de Montgomery in 1084.

This station was built on the site of the Abbey Refectory. Most of the outbuildings of the Abbey had been demolished by Telford when he diverted the approach of the main road into Shrewsbury to the south of the Abbey church, an act of officially sanctioned vandalism that saved barely a minute on the tight schedules of the Mail coaches. A surviving remnant, the Refectory pulpit, looked over the new station yard. The station was reached by a branch off what was meant as the main line at Coleham Junction, at the bottom of the climb leading to the Potteries Junction with the Wellington line. Plans for a triangular junction here never materialised. The branch followed the Rea Brook before crossing it on a girder bridge to enter the station itself. Despite the formation of the bigger Potteries, Shrewsbury & North Wales Railway there seemed to be little money to spare for the station; it was a humble affair, consisting of two low platforms and a single storey red-brick building, with yellow brick decorations, housing the station office, the booking office, waiting room and

Above:
Shropshire & Montgomeryshire signs outside Shrewsbury (Abbey) station in 1911.
L&GRP courtesy David & Charles

Below:
A Shropshire & Montgomeryshire train arriving at Shrewsbury (Abbey) in the 1920s.
Ian Allan Library

Top:
Ex-LNWR 'Coal' engine still carrying its LMS number 8236 with two of the ex-Midland carriages, c1933 at the Abbey station.
Lens of Sutton

Above:
Shunting oil tankers at the Abbey terminal in April 1983. *Author*

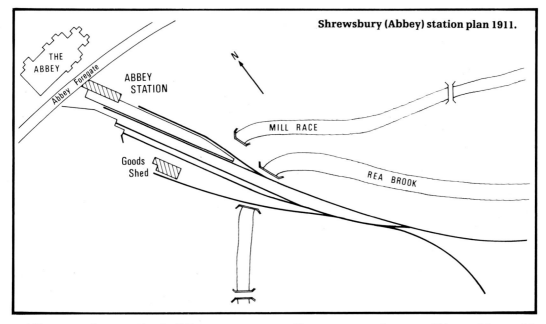

public conveniences. The building sported a narrow wooden canopy that was more for ornament than for any protection against the elements, and on this was painted 'Abbey Station'. There was also a goods yard nearby. The station had changed little by the time of the closure of 1880, and the Shropshire Railways did not touch the buildings. By the time it took over the line these were used as stables and as a coal merchants office, the whole of the platform area being used for coal storage. It was rented by a Joseph Crane for just £15 per annum.

The Shropshire Railways did try to improve the rail access to the station, which had been subjected to flooding and also had a steep gradient leading out of it. The engine shed and carriage shed to the south were demolished, the track level raised by new earth-works, and the girder bridge over the Rea Brook was replaced by a wide brick arched structure capable of carrying about six lines of railway with ease. After the new company ran out of money to carry on the work the station continued to fall into disrepair through neglect and ill-use. By the turn of the century most of the woodwork was rotted, the vandalised parapet of the new approach bridge lay at the bottom of the Rea with the girders of the old, and the area around Coleham Junction was a municipal rubbish tip. In addition, the adjacent Midland Railway-Carriage & Wagon Co had tipped all its rubbish on to the station branch line as well, and the tracks were buried in cinders.

Never a man to buy new if he could use old, Stephens found the brickwork of the station building to be fairly sound and so set about renovating it as his Shropshire & Montgomeryshire terminus. The rotting canopy was replaced by a much more substantial shelter resting on wooden pillars, and new advertising hoardings announcing the railway's existence were put up by the Abbey Foregate. The old platforms had disappeared and in any case were not at the right level for the new approach. A new island platform was built slightly to the south of the site of the originals which was 230ft long, 10ft wide and 3ft above the level of the tracks. A water tower was built at the southern end of the platform which was also given a set of standard lamps. A larger water tower stood on a girder frame just outside the station, and there was also a goods crane nearby built by the Abbey Works just over the boundary fence. This station was simply called Shrewsbury, but appeared in timetables as Shrewsbury Abbey, or the Abbey Station, Shrewsbury.

After the line had closed again in 1933 the station buildings continued in use as offices for the goods traffic that still used the station and the station yard. Later, a line of rickety wagons stood on one side of the island platform used as storage spaces. In the early years of World War 2 the buildings were used for a time for ARP practices, and the Army didn't actually take them over until 1944. Under Army control the lamps on the platforms disappeared and most of the fittings

followed suit; a few of the noticeboards (some of London & North Western origin, another from the London, Chatham & Dover Railway) survived the war but most had gone before the closure of 1960. The east side of the island platform was cleared of track in the 1950s, but the station remained open for goods traffic till 1968. The station sidings were still used by the tankers using the oil depot next to the site until that depot was modernised and a new siding laid in the early 1970s. The station site is now occupied by a builders' merchant which was founded by the son of one of the station masters at the Abbey station; the platform is used for storing building materials on, and there is a fence down the middle of it. The original station buildings survive and now

serve as something for larger pieces of building material to lean against. The collection of wooden huts in the station site mostly date from the Shropshire & Montgomeryshire era as well. Incidentally, the platform water tower was dismantled and taken to the Tenterden Railway Society, which has restored a section of another of the Colonel Stephens' light railways — the Kent & East Sussex.

Shrewsbury has never really been large enough to support commuter traffic and none of the original companies built stations in the suburbs. There were local demands for stations in Coleham and at Bayston Hill on the Hereford line in the 1850s but the company turned them down, despite considering closing Condover station at one point and building one in between that village and Bayston Hill. All the surrounding villages on or near the railways were well served by stations in any case.

The 'Potts' was at one time going to build a station at Red Hill Junction to interchange

Above:

**Hookagate Halt on the Shropshire &
Montgomeryshire Railway. Formerly Hookagate
& Redhill, it replaced a previous PS&NWR
station nearby called Red Hill.** *Lens of Sutton*

passengers with the Welshpool line. When the junction was abandoned and the deviation line built, the company opened a station nevertheless, presumably hoping to capitalise on the excursion traffic to what was then a popular picnic spot — the company didn't seem troubled by the fact that the owners of the Welshpool line hadn't bothered to open such a station themselves. The original Red Hill station was of two masonry platforms fitted out with wooden buildings, a standard pattern for the stations along the rest of the line, and was reached by a track off the lane from Shrewsbury-Hookagate. After the line was singled the northern (or up) set of tracks was lifted along with the up platform. The remaining platform was 180ft long and had steps at each end rather than the usual ramps. After closure the station suffered in the period of dereliction along with the rest of the line. By the end of the century the station buildings had virtually disappeared, and by the time the Shropshire & Montgomeryshire took over the

platform had gone as well, no doubt quarried for building stone by the locals.

The new company rebuilt the station a hundred yards or so nearer to Shrewsbury, but in a much simpler fashion than before. Really a halt, the new station was just a wooden platform south of the line, fitted out with the standard Shropshire & Montgomeryshire fittings of a wooden shelter-cum-booking office, a lamp, a fence and a nameboard. It was renamed Hookagate & Redhill after May 1921 and was just called Hookagate by the time it had closed in 1933. It was still used for the occasional goods traffic until the war, but the Army demolished it completely in preparation for the building of the Hookagate Exchange Sidings at the start of 1941.

Above:
Meole Brace station was the main ticket collecting station for trains approaching Shrewsbury (Abbey) in early years, and was one of the few to remain staffed until the end of passenger traffic. *Lens of Sutton*

Centre right:
Meole Brace was also the starting point for several excursions in the late 1930s. Here recently restored No 1 *Gazelle* waits at the start of such a trip on 14 October 1939. The wagon behind is in Meole Brace's coal sidings.
Graham Vincent

Bottom right:
A Conditional Stop platform signal at Edgebold station. In this position trains had to stop. When side-on, trains went past without stopping.
Real Photos

Like all of Colonel Stephens' light railways, the Shropshire & Montgomeryshire built stations and halts wherever it thought they could attract passengers, however few. Between Hookagate & Redhill and the Abbey station the company opened two more stations in 1911. The first was at Meole Brace, sheltered under a road bridge. Built in the standard pattern of the line it was a single platform south of the line, but it also boasted a siding, mainly used for coal. It became the ticket collection point for trains approaching Shrewsbury, and was one of the few stations on the line to remain staffed in the drastic economies needed in the 1920s; it was also one of the few not to become 'conditional stop' stations, and survived for goods traffic until the line's closure. The other station was in Belle Vue, another standard pattern construction sheltering under the main road to Hereford, south of the line just before it veered away from the Welshpool line to cross over the Hereford and Severn Valley lines to reach the Abbey station. It was actually opened after the others on the line, in September 1911. It was known locally as Belle Vue Platform for a while, but its official name was Shrewsbury West. It was an odd place to put a station; once the waiting for the train had been taken into account, and the time taken to walk from the Abbey station into the town centre, it was much quicker to walk down the Belle Vue Road. Indeed, many of the people who did use Shrewsbury West got off here in preference to the Abbey station to save time. It closed along with the rest of the line's stations in November 1933 and there was no real goods traffic to keep it open; in any case it had been unmanned early on. The bridge under which the station stood was built by the 'Potts' next to a bridge built by the Welshpool company; the 'Potts' bridge was knocked down after the closing of the line in 1960 to improve the visibility on what is now the A49. Interestingly, the end building in the row of houses nearby has a diagonal end wall which followed the former boundary of the railway company.

Until the opening of the Shrewsbury & Hereford line the signalling requirements in Shrewsbury were quite small, but then a signalbox had to be built at the new junction, originally called Wellington Junction but later renamed Severn Bridge Junction. It was of a rather unusual half-timbered design at the south end of the bridge. A second signalbox was needed at Crewe Junction when the Crewe line opened, and another at Sutton Bridge to control the two junctions off the Hereford line. A whistle code was in force here, with one, two or three whistles required of engines coming in from the Severn Valley, Hereford or Welshpool lines. In addition, a green light had to be displayed on the buffer beam of engines working in from the Severn Valley and the Welshpool lines at night time. The signals in Shrewsbury were all of the slotted semaphore type, mostly replaced by more modern semaphores at the end of the 1880s.

The opening of the Abbey Curve required two more signalboxes at English Bridge and Abbey Foregate Junctions, and further boxes were required to control the various goods yards; in 1880 the station was resignalled and a new signal-cum-points box was built on the Severn viaduct over the tracks. The telegraph was installed on the Shrewsbury & Birmingham and the Shrewsbury & Chester lines by 1852 and the Hereford line had been similarly treated by the 1860s. Little is known of the signalling on the Potteries line, except that semaphore signals were used and it had at least one signalbox, at Coleham Junction; this was made of wood and had disappeared by 1902.

Below:
Severn Bridge Junction signalbox is one of the largest on BR but is threatened with demolition in the very near future. Here Class 47 No 47.519 heads a train from Euston past the box into Shrewsbury in January 1985. *Author*

The rebuilding of the General station between 1899-1902 saw a radical resignalling programme. The 1880 box was dismantled and replaced by the present LNWR-pattern Severn Bridge Junction box, which with 180 levers is now the largest manual box in Britain. Another large box was needed at Crewe Junction, having 120 levers, and a new Central Cabin box was built at the head of the island bay platforms to control internal workings inside the station. The Light Railways Act only required signals at junctions or main stations, so the Shropshire & Montgomeryshire only had signals in Shrewsbury at the Abbey station and at Meole Brace Exchange sidings, the latter controlled by a new signalbox next to the Welshpool line. This closed when the sidings did and was demolished about 1948. The Shropshire & Montgomeryshire introduced its own variety of platform signal, a diamond, to turn against trains if passengers wanted them to halt at conditional-stop stations.

The rebuilding of the station again in the early 1960s entailed a re-locking of the Severn Bridge box which lost several of its levers and took over the work of the old Central Cabin. The signalbox at Coleham was due for replacement in 1965 and a new one next to it had just reached foundation height when the Coton Hill (South) box was demolished in a fatal accident. The frame destined for the new Coleham box was refitted into the rebuilt one at Coton Hill and the Coleham box was never finished. The semaphore signals at Shrewsbury are a mixture of upper and lower quadrants, but the Great Western pattern predominate. There were two starter colour signals, put up for the island platform bays, and another colour light protects the approach from the Rea Viaduct to the station. At present there is a radical plan to modernise completely all the local signalling which will involve demolishing the old manual boxes, dismantling the impressive semaphore gantries and replacing them all with colour light signals controlled from a central power box at the station itself. This will coincide with the proposed singling of the Chester line. The Welshpool line through to Aberystwyth is due to be converted to radio-signalling controlled by a radio-centre at Machynlleth.

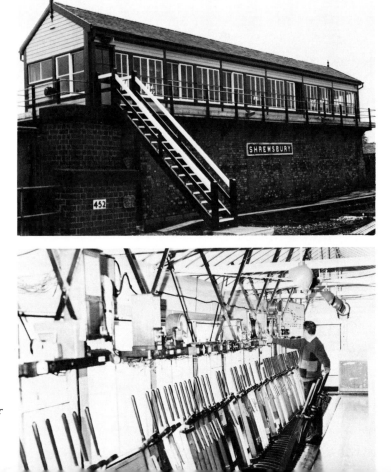

Above right:
Crewe Junction signalbox in November 1984. *Author*

Right:
Inside Crewe Junction signalbox in November 1984. Some of the instruments go back to the turn of the century, a mixture of GWR, LNWR, LMSR and BR! *Author*

4 The Development of Goods Traffic

Shrewsbury is not an industrial town, and never really has been one. It has, however, always been the major market town for the region, and as it developed as a railway junction it expanded into an important rail goods distribution centre for the local agricultural industry; it was also a place where goods traffic bound to and from elsewhere passed through, stopping only to perhaps change engines or to inspect wagons. The first goods depot was built by the Shrewsbury & Chester Railway off its main line just north of the station and was reached from Castle Foregate, which gave the depot its name. It consisted at first of just a few sidings and a Brassey-built warehouse but expanded rapidly. The Great Western found the site too small for its growing needs and built a new yard east of the main line north of the Ellesmere Road bridge, which was called Coton Hill. Later still more sidings were laid opposite the Coton Hill yard and the two yards became Coton Hill (North) and Coton Hill (South). The original warehouse was rebuilt and extended several times, particularly at the turn of the century when the size of the building was doubled by building an extension northwards in the same style as the old. This had a central platform with rail access on the one side, and access for road vehicles on the other, and there were the usual goods offices, and weighbridge and a weighbridge clerks office. The Crewe line was carried over the depot's Castle Foregate entrance on a girder bridge. At around the turn of the century the Great Western added another public siding — Greenfields siding — with access off the Ellesmere Road.

The Shropshire Union naturally built its goods depot on its own land; the Union owned the Shrewsbury Canal and built the depot next to its terminal basin off Howard Street; this was reached by a single-line spur from the station which remained an inconvenient entrance until the depot closed. There were new warehouses built at the northern end of the depot later, and part of the canal basin was filled in to make more room for extra sidings. In 1857 the London & North Western bought the adjacent Butter Market, a fine neo-classical structure of 1836, and converted it into a grain warehouse which it remained for many years.

The Shrewsbury & Birmingham built its goods depot east of the Underdale Road and south of the line. The Shropshire Union had a depot on the opposite side of the line but it would appear that the two yards were worked jointly from the start, and they certainly were from 1864 when the Joint Traffic Committee was set up. Rather confusingly the depot was called Abbey Foregate goods depot, although

Left:
Howard Street Warehouse — originally built in 1836 as the Butter Market. The unusual alignment is due to rebuilding after the station nearby was enlarged in 1899-1902. *Author*

the Abbey Foregate was over a hundred yards away. In later years the southern side of the yard concentrated mainly on coal traffic, and the side north of the line was often used for traffic to and from the Shrewsbury Shows — particularly horses arriving for them and also for the Shrewsbury Races. For some reason the Shrewsbury & Hereford built its depot at Coleham, which was then just an area of fields away from the town centre. Brassey constructed it and estimated that 8,000sq yd of earth was needed to raise up the level of the yard and 1,400 sleepers were needed to take 75 tons of rails attached by 30 tons of track-chairs. Twelve points were needed, three wagon turntables, a weighbridge and a five-ton crane; the estimated cost was £6,937.

The other briefly independent line, the West Midland, shared the Great Western's Castle Foregate depot. The London & North Western quickly found the Shropshire Union yard too small and built a new depot, called simply enough the New Yard, off Castle Foregate and connected to its Crewe line. It was separated from the Great Western's Castle Foregate yard by the Bagley Brook. Much later, in the days of

Above:
'28XX' class 2-8-0 No 3813 on a South Wales to the North goods at Condover on 26 July 1941.
Peter Clay/LoS

the London, Midland & Scottish, sorting sidings were added at Harlescott; there were also other sorting sidings added at Sutton Bridge on the Hereford line (the Shelf Sidings). In 1864 the goods yard at Coleham and Abbey Foregate came under the control of the stationmaster at the Joint station. It was the custom to have red and black days for dispatching goods to places that could be reached in about the same time by both the Great Western and London & North Western companies so that there could be no accusations of favouritism by the staff, each company having the traffic on alternate days.

The Potteries, Shrewsbury & North Wales Railway had a small goods yard by its own Abbey station, but also had a larger yard at the junction with the Wellington line; called the Potteries Junction yard it was mainly used for exchanging traffic to and from the joint line, and was controlled by a signalbox opposite the junction; there was also a small goods warehouse.

The proper development of goods traffic inevitably suffered because of the inter-company wars of the 1850s. The Shrewsbury & Chester lamented that 'the through goods traffic continues to be impeded by the hostile proceedings and arrangements of the London & North Western and the Birkenhead companies', but the same meeting of Directors was told that local goods traffic was steadily increasing. It is not hard to see how the London & North Western could stifle the through traffic. Passengers may have been unwilling to take a longer way round, even if it was cheaper, but consigners of goods were not interested in speed, just cost. The London & North Western could cut tolls and re-route traffic at will using its line and those of subject companies. On the important Midlands to the Mersey route the company had little trouble keeping most of the traffic on its own railway; after all it controlled each end of the Shrewsbury companies' rival route, delaying the Stour Valley line in the south and dominating the Birkenhead Railway in the north. Undeterred, the 'Fighting Shrewsburies' did fight back. The Shrewsbury & Chester acquired the steamer *Taliesin* in November 1849 to work flat-bottomed barges on the Dee for the company's goods carrying, and hired a second steamer the following year. The Shrewsbury & Birmingham built new wharves on the Birmingham Canal (not without a fight — literally) to carry traffic on into Birmingham. But the transhipments and extra costs were a very expensive way of doing battle. The London & North Western also attacked the goods traffic between Shrewsbury and the Midlands using the Shropshire Union line in complete disregard of written agreements to the contrary. Once the Shrewsbury & Hereford line was ready, the London & North Western routed traffic off the then subject Newport, Abergavenny & Hereford line to the Mersey by way of Shrewsbury, the Shropshire Union and its own line to Liverpool. Finally the price-cutting and re-routing ceased and by 1854 the Shrewsbury companies had unhindered access to Birmingham, and the first through freight trains from there along the Shrewsbury lines to Birkenhead started on 2 February 1856. The attack on the Shrewsbury & Chester's and Shrewsbury & Birmingham's goods traffic was totally unwarranted; they had never intended cutting goods rates in the first place.

Shrewsbury had two main markets, one for general produce and one for livestock. In the early part of the 19th century the livestock market was the streets of Shrewsbury, especially those around the old Market Square. It was then decided to build a new livestock market on a purpose-built site and the Raven Meadows were drained. This site was chosen in preference to one at Abbey Foregate mainly because of the nearby station, and a new road — Smithfield Road — was built to connect it with the station. This new livestock market was opened in November 1850 and for over a century the cattle traffic was a very important part of Shrewsbury's goods traffic. Each of the main goods depots had cattle pens and cattle loading platforms and there were regular market day trains to and from the town. The gradual increase in road haulage and the unsuitability of rail travel for livestock led to the virtual elimination of cattle trains in the 1960s; in any case the livestock market in Shrewsbury was then moved to its new site at Harlescott and although this new Smithfield is next to the Crewe line, it has no rail connection. One important product of cattle is of course milk; for many years until the 1950s there was a daily milk train from the large dairy at Dorrington (just south of Shrewsbury) to Marylebone in London, and there were also milk trains serving dairies at Minsterley and at Whittington. Other livestock was carried by railway, notably horses to and from the once famous Shrewsbury horse fairs, but cattle were by far the most important.

The opening of the railways led to new and expanding markets for local farm produce, with grain and sugar beet providing important revenue for the railway companies. The sugar

Above:
'Hall' class 4-6-0s were the largest locomotives allowed to work the northern portion of the Severn Valley line. No 4959 *Purley Hall* leaves Sutton Bridge with a coal train, presumably bound for Buildwas power station on 2 June 1942. *Peter Clay/LoS*

beet traffic was particularly important to the Shropshire & Montgomeryshire company, anxious for any traffic it could get, and in the beet season trainloads of the crops would pass through the exchange sidings at Meole. The traffic lasted until the end of the line in 1960. Sugar beet traffic from all over Shropshire was once taken by rail to the Allscott sugar mill a few miles east of Shrewsbury which had its own standard gauge internal railway to deal with the arriving traffic. In the early 1980s this system was abandoned and all traffic to and from the mill now goes by road.

As well as providing an outlet for local farmers, the railways also made farming necessities easier to obtain, and cheaper to buy. All of the goods depots in Shrewsbury could offer for sale such things as 'Salt, Lime, Linseed Cake and Best Peruvian Guano'.

Apart from agriculture the other local industry most affected by the developing

Above:
The Shelf Sidings at Sutton Bridge in 1959, with wagons everywhere.
Russel Mulford/Michael Embrey

Below:
'Patriot' 4-6-0 No 45542 leaves Coleham Goods and joins the main line before heading south with a mixed goods train in 1955.
Russel Mulford/Michael Embrey

Above:
ROD 2-8-0 No 3040 trundles past Little Stretton on a South Wales to the North goods train on 7 August 1954. *Donald Kelk*

railways was that of mining and quarrying. Lead, limestone and coal were all important exports from Shropshire and the nearby parts of Wales in the 19th century and the railways provided the only practical means of transport. Most of the coal mines were in east or north Shropshire, but there was a small coalfield just to the west of Shrewsbury near Hanwood, and the Short Hill Colliery was handily placed between the Welshpool and Minsterley lines at Cruckmeole Junction and had its own small rail-linked internal system of track. A plan to build a line to it from the Potteries, Shrewsbury & North Wales line never came to fruition, but this company did served lime kilns just to the west of its Red Hill station; these seem to have closed soon after the line, in the 1880s.

The lead mines in the Stiperstones area of Western Shropshire were enjoying a brief revival in the 1870s and a rail link to connect up with the main lines at Shrewsbury was needed. The nearest line running into the town

was the Minsterley branch line, and in 1877 a narrow gauge mineral line was opened from Snailbeach to this line at exchange sidings near Pontesbury. This was the Snailbeach District Railways (sic) but traffic was erratic and fell off rapidly at the end of the century causing the line to close in 1915. It was re-opened by Colonel Stephens, always a lover of lost causes, in 1923 hoping to serve the roadstone quarries at Callow and some baryte traffic from the old lead mine spoil heaps, but closed again in 1947. The amount of traffic generated by that time was negligible.

The Potteries, Shrewsbury & North Wales Railway in particular relied on the roadstone traffic from the quarries on its branches to Nantmawr and to Criggion, and most of this traffic was routed by way of Shrewsbury to

Above:
A busy scene at Sutton Bridge in 1958, with Standard 5 No 73013 heading a heavy goods past 0-6-0PT No 3782 whose train of oil tankers and coal trucks is probably bound for the Abbey terminus. *Russel Mulford/Michael Embrey*

join trains of the Great Western or London & North Western at the Potteries Junction yard. In 1872 the company carried 88,813 tons of mineral traffic, mainly roadstone, but by 1877 the amount was just 16,767 tons, and it was this dramatic fall off in revenue that helped close down the line. It also meant that the mineral trains to the Potteries yard became less and less frequent, and the daily train in the working timetables would often not run for weeks. Ironically, on one of the rarer appearances of this mineral train the Potteries suffered one of its very few fatal accidents. On 16 October 1875 a London & North Western goods train was shunting in the Potteries yard, which by this time had been unofficially taken over by the two Joint companies — the 'Potts' couldn't even afford a marshal at the yard to stop them. Three wagons standing at the bottom end of the yard were knocked over the scotch-blocks and ran down the incline towards Bell Lane, a not uncommon occurrence as there were no catch points at these

sidings. Unfortunately one of the mineral trains was at that moment passing the long-disused signal guarding the line as it trundled up the cutting to the bridge under the Abbey Foregate road. The train consisted of 14 mineral wagons hauled by a six-coupled tank engine running bunker first. The driver saw the wagons but could do nothing, and in the collision they and six of the mineral wagons, along with the locomotive, were derailed and the driver was caught between the bunker and the firebox, dying later of his injuries. At the inquiry it was revealed that the 'Potts' seldom used brake vans and the brakesman on such a mineral train had to leap from wagon to wagon applying each individual brake.

When the Shropshire & Montgomeryshire re-opened the line it too relied to a large extent on the mineral traffic, mainly from Criggion, as the Nantmawr branch had by that time been taken over by the Cambrian Railways. This traffic kept the line open after passenger traffic had ceased. There is a slight irony in the fact that the increased demand for roadstone was due entirely to the new road-building programmes that were directly putting the line out of business. One important contract of the quarries was the supply of stone for the East Lancs Road, during which time several trains a day rumbled into the exchange sidings at Meole Brace. The quarry traffic survived right up until the end of the line, running into the new yard at Hookagate after 1941.

The local Permanent Way District at Shrewsbury still gets its ballast from the area once served by the Nantmawr branch, with a daily train hauled by a diesel stabled at Shrewsbury running as required by a roundabout way through Gobowen and Oswestry to reach the quarries. This is despite a more recent quarrying development just south of Shrewsbury at Bayston Hill. The stone from here is taken for use as ballast mainly by the northwestern areas of the railways, and several trains a day ply between the quarries

and Guide Bridge, Manchester. These are hauled by locomotives specially fitted to work slowly through the quarry company's loading plant. As there is no through loop, trains have to be reversed in off the main Hereford line from a ground frame, and locomotives have to run round their trains further on down the line at the disused station at Dorrington.

The railways also generated their own local industries. In Shrewsbury these ranged from the small factory of Potters Brothers in Frankwell making tarpaulins for railway trucks, to the large factory built by the Midland Railway-Carriage & Wagon Company which bought Richard France's former contractors yard between the Abbey station and the Coleham locomotive depots in 1877. The factory grew into a large installation of workshops, paintshops and offices. Through the main factory building ran no less than 11 lines of track connected by a turntable at the southern end. There were also rail links to storage sidings on the other side of the Rea

Below:
2-6-0 No 6310 passing Shrewsbury sheds with a goods for South Wales on 12 September 1961.
Ian Allan Library

Above:
Ivatt 2-6-2T No 41304 on a Ruabon-Shrewsbury pick-up goods at Crewe Junction on 24 April 1964. *Derek Cross*

Brook next to the Abbey Foregate, and rail sidings leading to the 'Potts' line at its terminus, and to the Coleham sheds above. The company concentrated originally on the building, repairing and leasing of private owner wagons for the railways, but later diversified into other fields: one of its specialities was carriage and wagon stock for narrow gauge railways, supplying the Vale of Rheidol Railway and all the rolling stock for the Glyn Valley Tramway in 1888. For the latter it built 14 coaches and over 200 mineral wagons; the coaches were to the same basic design, of wooden bodies and frames and all being four-wheelers 14ft 3in long. The mineral wagons were mainly four-tonners some 10ft 8in in length. Most of the rolling stock supplied to the Tramway was still running when it closed in 1935. The carriages supplied to the Vale of Rheidol were 17 bogie coaches in 1902 built for the twisty line up to Devil's Bridge, some 32ft long with wooden frames. They also supplied some goods wagons for the line as well. The largest carriages built by the company were the 45ft bogie carriages built for the Cambrian Railways between 1895 and 1903. The company was also involved in the manufacture of trams, including horse-drawn examples and tram trailers for steam trams;

its vehicles found their way all over Britain, and some even were exported to Delhi. It was the pioneer of electric tramcars, and was the first commercial builder in Britain to produce them in 1882 when it supplied trams, trailers and trucks for the Giants Causeway Tramway. The company also built the famous Blackpool 'Dreadnoughts'. In 1912 the works were transferred to larger premises in Birmingham, and the company later became part of the giant Metro-Cammell group, although it retained its independence on paper until being wound up in 1948.

Much of the goods traffic dealt with by Shrewsbury was actually passing through it on the trunk routes that met in the town. The most important traffic for well over a century was that of coal, not only brought in to be used by the industrial and domestic users in the town, but passing through from South Wales on the way to the Mersey. Each of the goods depots did have a supply of coal merchants. Joseph Crane had started in business in 1868

Above left:
Britannia Pacific No 70020 *Mercury* on a 'C' class goods at Crewe Junction on 21 July 1954.
Brian Morrison

Left:
4-6-0 No 6901 *Arley Hall* leaves Shrewsbury with a heavy goods on 23 June 1962 heading for the south. *D. I. Wood*

Above right:
Stanier 2-8-0 No 48419 approaching Bayston Hill heading south on 24 September 1961.
M. Mensing

and within a few years had coal depots at the Abbey Foregate, Abbey Station and Castle Foregate yards. The 'all important distribution of coal' played an important part in the traffic planning of local railway companies, which of course used vast quantities themselves. As late as 1974 a new Coal Concentration Plant was opened in the New York goods depot off Castle Foregate, capable of handling 60,000 tons a year off-loaded from railway coal hoppers in the siding. A usual train consists of 15 25-ton hopper wagons, and the coal is taken on by lorry.

As the 20th century progressed so the demand for oil increased rapidly. After World War 1 the local firm of Morris's purchased large quantities of surplus oil from the Government and rented the disused Midland Railway-Carriage & Wagon Co's factory to store it in; the factory then belonged to the Great Western which had acquired it hoping to expand the Railway's siding and repair capacity — a plan never carried through. By the late 1920s Morris's opened its own oil depot in the New Yard, and today this has been redeveloped as a sophisticated plant capable of off-loading up to 10,000gal an hour from oil tanker wagons in the siding and then pumping it through pipes to the main bulk storage tanks at the northern end of the former Shropshire Union yard.

In 1933 the Anglo-American Oil Co built a depot by the side of the Abbey station, and traffic to it off the Shropshire & Montgomery-shire started in the following year. In 1936 the plant was expanded to cater for the 'Essolube' products. The tankers reached the plant originally by way of the Meole Brace Exchange Sidings, but after the Hookagate yard was built, the tankers were marshalled there. With the closure of the rest of the line in 1960, the oil traffic was saved by the construction of a short spur to the Severn Valley line. The daily tanker service to this Abbey oil terminal is as eccentric as any in the 'Potts' history. The tankers, usually four or five, are collected at the Coton Hill (North) yard; from here other tanker trains go to depots at Whittington and to Aberystwyth. After passing through the station with its load, the duty shunter hauls them across the Rea Viaduct — at this point they are barely 200yd from their destination. The little train then ignores the Severn Valley junction, passes the Sutton Bridge signalbox and the junction for Welshpool before reversing into the Shelf Sidings off the Hereford line. The shunter runs round the tankers and then hauls them back past the two junctions and on to a long siding by the site of Coleham sheds. From here on it will be the only locomotive on the line so no signals are needed; it propels the tankers on to the Severn Valley line to the 1960 junction of the new spur. Just past here the Severn Valley itself has been cut short by a new inner ring road, but there is enough left to form a short shunting neck into which the train is put; the shunter then hauls the train over the spur and on to the old line down to the Abbey. After a few shunting manoeuvres the shunter extracts the empty tankers from the unloading siding at the plant and replaces them with the fresh ones, after which the empties return to Coton Hill by the same roundabout route; sometimes the shunter is called on to visit Hookagate with empty bolster wagons and usually takes the empty tanker wagon along. The future of this service has been under threat since its inception, but most of the rotting sleepers were renewed in 1983 and perhaps it will last a while longer; the latest plans are to remove the depot to Coton Hill.

The most important through traffic for much of the 19th century was undoubtedly the 'considerable Mineral traffic, from the interchange of Red Ore from Birkenhead for the Iron Masters of South Wales, with Steam Coals back from that district to the River Mersey'. This traffic had started in the late 1850s and

Left:
Meole Brace Exchange Sidings between the S&MR and the Welshpool line, c1911. *Real Photos*

Below:
S&MR No 3 *Hesperus* with the daily goods from Shrewsbury (Abbey) station in 1937.
Lens of Sutton

Above:
A Webb 0-6-2 'Coal' Tank shunting in the Meole Brace Exchange Sidings on 31 July 1941. The oil tank wagon will probably be from the Abbey terminal, while the absence of mineral wagons is due to the temporary closure of the Criggion branch at this time. These sidings would shortly be replaced by new ones at Hookagate.
Graham Vincent

Right:
The new sidings at Hookagate under construction on 29 June 1941, looking east. The Welshpool line is on the left. *Graham Vincent*

was originally worked by the Newport, Abergavenny & Hereford Railway by agreement with the other companies involved. After its amalgamation with the West Midland Railway the Great Western monopolised the traffic and in 1866 had nine trains daily trundling through Shrewsbury heading north with coal and returning with iron-ore. As the 'interchange' was not quite balanced, and more coal went north than iron ore went south, long trains of empty private owners' coal wagons passed through Shrewsbury back to the collieries. The London & North Western began its own coal trains from South Wales in the 1870s. The iron ore traffic dwindled, especially as the ports of South Wales were developed, but the coal traffic continued for over a hundred years.

By the 1920s the Great Western had improved its long-distance goods handling by introducing fast night services and express goods trains. In 1899 there had been just one train designated as 'Express Goods' passing through Shrewsbury, the 10.20am from Liverpool to the Midlands, and one train classed as a 'Special Goods', the 7.05am from Hollinswood terminating at Coton Hill (North). By 1929 Shrewsbury was the destination of one of the fastest goods trains of the Great Western, the 10.30pm from Greenford which took just 3hr 43min on its non-stop run of over 145 miles. In 1929 the company started naming its night-time good expresses, and such services as 'The Feeder' (6.05pm Birkenhead-Pontypool Road), 'The Meat' (3.55pm Birkenhead-Smithfield), 'The Spud' (9.45pm Cardiff-Saltney) and the 'Flying Skipper' (12.45pm Wolverhampton-Birkenhead) passed through Shrewsbury in the early hours. The London Midland & Scottish didn't have many long distance freights passing through Shrewsbury apart from the coal trains and the goods between Shrewsbury and Swansea. In 1946 Shrewsbury was chosen as the Great

Top:
A busy scene at Hookagate on 1 April 1947. Engines in various states of decay include WD Nos 70093, 70095, 70099 and 70097 (all 'Dean Goods') with WD Nos 8182, 8108 and 8236 (all ex-S&MR); another 'Dean Goods', WD 70196, passes with old carriages used for transporting railway staff and troops along the line.
Graham Vincent

Above:
A 'Dean Goods' passes Edgebold (ex-Hanwood Road) station on the S&MR with a goods bound for Hookagate in 1947. *Peter Clay/LoS*

Western's centre for its short-lived zonal system.

The rapid advances of road transport in the postwar years effectively killed off the pick-up goods trains and made large goods yards such as those in Shrewsbury redundant. There were plans in the late 1950s to replace all the yards in the area with a new marshalling yard that was originally to be built just east of the Belvidere Bridge — later re-planned for Walcot, just outside Wellington — but this idea was scrapped in 1960. Beeching did propose at one point a liner-train service on the Birmingham-Birkenhead line with Shrewsbury the liner-terminal for Central and North Wales, but in the published British Railways plan for goods traffic 1965 the route was not one listed for future development. The goods depots began to be closed down. Coleham yard was closed on 15 August 1966 and the site was taken over by the local permanent way office as its main depot. Abbey Foregate yard closed on 10 October 1968, and is now built over, and was followed by the Shropshire Union yard in Howard Street which was closed on 5 April 1971 and is now a car park. Greenfield siding closed on 6 May 1968.

World War 2 was to change radically the old 'Potts'; apart from the mineral traffic the line had just one goods train a day prewar; often

Above:
Class 25 No 25.201 heads for Bayston Hill quarries with an empty train and approaches Sutton Bridge in April 1982. *Author*

Below:
A Class 47 takes its train through the rapid loading plant at Bayston Hill quarry in June 1984. *Author*

little more than a single ex-Midland Railway van behind an ageing *Hesperus*. However, the Army needed extra sidings and yards to cope with the wartime ammunition traffic from its new depots. The main marshalling yard was at Ford, near the Shrawardine Bridge over the Severn, but at Hookagate it built a large yard to serve as exchange sidings with the Welshpool line, to act as reception and dispatch sidings for trains arriving and departing on the main line. The site was cleared by January 1941 and work was started on laying the sidings with flat-bottomed track. There were four main sidings each about 500yd long, together with a set of three shorter sidings that acted as an engine depot of sorts, complete with inspection pit, water tower and coaling stage. By July the work was nearly finished and the connecting spur to the Welshpool line was put in, controlled by a new signalbox opposite the junction. Goods traffic on the line in the war years reached a peak of 349,986 tons, most of which was routed by way of Hookagate. Along with the 40,452 tons of civilian and mineral goods carried in the same year, 1943 was by far the best in the line's erratic history. At one time over 120 civilians were employed on the line; the Army made little use of the line to Abbey station except for liberty trains and collecting the occasional VIP. Inevitably, after the war the line was run down as the depots closed, and by 1959 the Army had little traffic left, and had no further use for Hookagate.

Top left:
In April 1982 a Class 40 with a full train of ballast hoppers heads north out of Shrewsbury past Crewe Bank signalbox en route from Bayston Hill quarries to Guide Bridge yard, Manchester.
Author

Left:
Permanent Way Department rolling stock outside Coleham depot in 1984. *Author*

Top
The Permanent Way Department, in the former Coleham goods depot, February 1985. *Author*

Above
The interior of the Midland Railway-Carriage & Wagon Works c1900. *Shropshire Libraries*

Above:
Unloading rails from the reception sidings at Hookagate Long-Rail Welding Depot in February 1985. *Author*

At the end of that year the Western Region began work on a new Long Rail Welding Depot on the site and this was ready by the summer. Originally it dealt with rails up to 300ft long, but now has the capacity to turn out rails 900ft long if required. Despite the transfer on the rest of the Shrewsbury area to the London Midland the depot has remained in Western Division hands, regarded by some as Paddington's 'West Berlin'. Most rails arrive at the Hookagate reception sidings in 60ft lengths: new ones now come from the British Steel Corporation's works at Workington, but rails from other sources, including France and West Germany, have been used in the past. The depot also deals in 'serviceable' rails, ones that have been used but still have enough life left in the unworn side to warrant re-laying on routes with fairly light traffic. After being off-loaded by the depot's shunter-propelled crane the rails begin their journey through the depot — the shunter is supplied by the London Midland at Shrewsbury. Under Western Region control the depot was given one of the

Region's small 0-6-0 Ruston & Hornsby diesel-electric shunters, PWM654, but now uses one of the Class 08s. Rails are taken through the depot on single-rail conveyers and the actual process is in a sort of squared-off horseshoe shape. After initial inspection the rails are barred on to the conveyers and taken to the first stage, the initial press shop where the rail ends are tested for alignment and if necessary straightened by a powerful press. Each individual cast number is recorded in a ledger in case of any future breakdown in service, and so each individual rail can be traced back to a particular date. Rails are then carried sideways by overhead gantry to start on more conveyers taking them through the main welding workshop and back to the rail-banks near to where they had arrived. 'Serviceable' rails have to have 2ft 6in cut off each end to get rid of the fish-plate bolt holes and go through a special sawing shop before being taken on the gantry. The spare ends are dumped in a nearby railway truck and taken away for scrap. Recently Hookagate has been using a revolutionary new device, the Precision Flame Rail Cutter, which can cut its way through a standard rail in seconds and has the added advantage of being portable. Before passing through the depot 'serviceable' rails have to be checked to make sure that they are the right way round for the welding process and for loading on to the trains that will take them to the relaying sites.

The ends of the rails have to be cleaned of rust and dirt because the welding process relies on a low voltage but a very high current,

so a good contact is vital. The rails enter the main welding shop, and once welding starts the process is semi-automatic. Strictly speaking this is not welding at all, as there are no additives involved: it is Flash Butt Upset Forge Welding, a variation — albeit highly sophisticated — of what village blacksmiths did for centuries. A brief burn off in the main welding machine gets rid of most impurities, and is followed by a preheating process in which the two rail ends are moved together and apart — a matter of millimetres while current is made and broken. Usually 14 such movements take place before the rail is ready. A brief flashing cycle with a sustained series of sparks gets rid of the remaining impurities and the rails are then butted together by powerful presses. The ends are not welded exactly level and there is a very slight rise at the joint to counteract any contraction later. A profile grinder then smoothes down the new join before the elongated rail passes through final assessment at a press similar to the first. All plant in these workshops is actually on rails, so that the machinery can be moved the right distance apart for the length of rail being welded. For

Left:
Demonstration of the new Precision Flame Rail Cutter at Hookagate in February 1985. *Author*

Below:
Inside the main welding shop at Hookagate, February 1985. *Author*

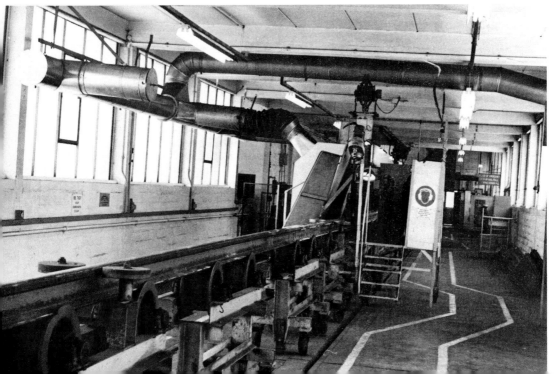

example, 'serviceable' rails are only 55ft long, not 60ft.

Once the rail has been checked it is transported to the rail banks to await loading on to the special trains that will take them to the re-laying sites. The rail bank is 1,400ft long with rail access on each side. A typical train will consist of 30 single bolster wagons with a barrier truck at the front to prevent damage to the locomotive and a roller truck at the back to help in unloading at the site. As there are no gantries on the rail banks, the rails — usually now 600ft long — are 'combed' and loaded into the trains with the help of a 'Cooch', a small mobile winch. Hookagate works one eight-hour shift but is of necessity an all-weather depot. At present its future is uncertain as British Rail is rationalising and modernising its rail welding plants, but as Hookagate has built up something of a reputation with experimental welding, on rails of chrome for example, and has also carried out experiments with special corrosion-resistant rail coatings, it may yet survive: it has already been reprieved once. It could perhaps survive by concentrating on welding 'serviceable' rails as well.

There is one remaining goods line to mention in Shrewsbury, one that only dates from 1932 but whose design goes back to the very beginnings of railways. In 1932 a new waterworks pumping station was built next to the River Severn near Shelton on the outskirts of Shrewsbury. At this point the river has cut deeply into the hillside and access to the new works was difficult, especially for heavier equipment. A small incline railway of about 2ft gauge was built down to the river; at the bottom a small turntable directed the small wagon used to a short extension running at right angles to the building itself. In 1943 Woodward & Co added a hand-operated winch drum and steel cable to the modernised system at the top of the incline and in 1978 this was converted to electric power and given the necessary safety covers. It is housed in a small brick shed just off the present A5, and is used about twice a year.

Shrewsbury is no longer an important centre for rail-borne goods traffic; only the Coton Hill (North) yard really sees much traffic, and most of the goods trains passing through Shrews-bury are doing just that, with oil, concrete and ballast trains making up the bulk of the traffic along with steel trains from South Wales.

Mail

Largely because of its position, Shrewsbury has always been an important part of the rail-borne postal system and even today has a regular mail train that leaves at 10.50pm every night travelling to York. This was not the first Travelling Post Office from Shrewsbury: as early as 1857 a TPO started running to Shrewsbury from the main London & North Western line at Tamworth starting at just before midnight. The train was mainly for the rural areas around Shrewsbury and later extended to Hereford, using a second coach. In March 1902 these two services were merged to become a Tamworth-Hereford TPO until being separated again in 1914. The original carriage was probably a 20ft six-wheel affair but was replaced by a 36ft six-wheeler in 1875; another vehicle 32ft long was supplied in 1887. In addition to these two sorting coaches there was a spare one kept at Shrewsbury, and in 1905 one of the older ones was replaced by a new 42-footer. The service stopped dealing with parcels in 1915 on account of the war, and stopped altogether on 28 February 1917.

Mail was carried on most of the local lines, but the only other sorting coach or TPO until the introduction of the York one was the Shrewsbury-Aberystwyth TPO started in 1883 and handled by the London & North Western. This quickly came under the control of Shrewsbury Post Office and in 1892 departed from Shrewsbury at 3.40am, arriving at Aberystwyth over the Cambrian Railways line at 7.25am; in the return direction it left Aberystwyth at 6pm, arriving in Shrewsbury at 9.50pm.

The Cambrian Railways built a combined letters and parcels sorting carriage in 1888 which was stationed at Shrewsbury after being replaced by a newer one in 1902; this carriage was suspended briefly during the war and was finally restored in 1919 running every night rather than the six weekdays as previously. It was suspended again in Septem-ber 1939 and has not been restarted.

The Shrewsbury & York TPO began in 1891 as a much different turn, working from Crewe to Shrewsbury to sort mail brought in on the mail train from the southwest, and was later diverted from Crewe to Normanton. In 1895 another sorting carriage from Bristol met the service at Shrewsbury. This became known as the Bristol, Shrewsbury & Normanton TPO, which left Bristol at 7.40pm, 40 minutes after the rival Midland Railway TPO, and in 1902 the northern section was extended to York. The Bristol coach was worked by men from Shrewsbury Post Office who went down on the 2.15am train from there. In fact it was the southbound Bristol, Shrewsbury & York TPO involved in the disaster at Shrewsbury station

Above:
Class 25 No 25.068 on a parcels train arriving at Shrewsbury station on 26 June 1976. *Kevin Lane*

in 1907. In 1910 the southern end of the route was changed to Cardiff, and in 1920 it was divided into Cardiff-Crewe and Shrewsbury-York sections, and the Shrewsbury-York has remained the same, except for some minor changes and a suspension in World War 2 ever since. In the early 1960s the old method of taking mail to the sorting office at Shrewsbury by van was replaced by a new continuous conveyor belt from the northern end of the station, carried over Howard Street in an enclosed bridge to the sorting offices opposite.

Sentinel

Work started on the Sentinel Factory in Harlescott in 1914. It was constructed by Alley & MacLellan's, a Scottish company which built steam road lorries and had found that most of its customers were in England. The housing estate opposite the works was also built by the

company to house its workers, and the houses were exceptionally well equipped for their time, each having such unheard of luxury as hot running water. By the early 1920s the company was considering putting its vertical boilered steam engines into railcars, and the first of these was built in 1923. They were exported after that all over the world, and ranged in gauge from 750mm to 5ft or more. One of the main early customers was the Delta Railway in Egypt which also bought some solo locomotives from the factory. The London, Midland & Scottish and the London & North Eastern companies each bought railcars with Sentinel engines, the carriages themselves

being built by Metro-Cammell of Birmingham: the early London, Midland & Scottish ones ended up on the Jersey Eastern Railway. The London & North Eastern bought many such railcars to work especially on the flat East Anglian branch lines.

The company developed a range of simple single and twin-geared shunting locomotives for railway use, and these too were exported in large numbers. The London & North Eastern was particularly fond of these and ordered many from 1927 onwards; they became its 'Y3' class and most survived to British Railways days. The company also supplied two unusual crane locomotives to the London & North Eastern to clear deposited ash at locomotive depots. The Sentinel company specialised in industrial locomotives and could usually adapt its basic designs to fit any requirements. Most of the locomotives were of 0-4-0 or 0-6-0 type, but there was at least one 0-6-0-0-6-0 articulated engine and an eight-coupled engine for the Army. Between 1923 and 1957 the company built over 850 engines. Their engines were seldom based at Shrewsbury shed; occasionally one would be based at the sub-shed at Ludlow to work the Clee Hill mineral lines.

In 1958 Rolls-Royce bought the 16-acre site for £1½million and although it did finish a few steam engines under construction, the company switched to the building of diesels. Most of these early Sentinel diesels were diesel-hydraulic 0-4-0s and 0-6-0s; later it built some 0-4-0 diesel mechanicals and a handful of diesel-electrics. Among the customers for these diesels were the Army (to which the company sent an 0-8-0), the Manchester Ship Canal, and the Port of Bristol Authority. Although over 200 diesels were built at the Sentinel Works, by the early 1970s all locomotive building was transferred to the then Rolls-Royce subsidiary Thomas Hill (Rotherham) Ltd, and the works only continued to make the engines. In 1984 the company was taken over by the giant Perkins Diesels empire which continues to build engines at the Harlescott factory.

ROLLS-ROYCE *reach double century*
the **200**th *Sentinel* DIESEL LOCOMOTIVE
this loco for STANTON and STAVELEY LIMITED

5 Locomotive Depots and Locomotives

None of the first four companies sharing the General station originally had their main locomotive depots in Shrewsbury, much to the annoyance of local businessmen. The Shrewsbury & Chester's main works was at Saltney and later became the main carriage works of the Great Western's Northern Division. The Shrewsbury & Birmingham built its works at Stafford Road, Wolverhampton, and this later became the main locomotive works of the Northern Division. The Shrewsbury & Hereford had its works near the Barrs Court station in Hereford, and the Shropshire Union was worked from the start by London & North Western locomotives based at Stafford.

Each company did have 'engine houses' in the town, however — the Shrewsbury & Birmingham and Shropshire Union having theirs on opposite sides of the joint line to Wellington just east of Underdale Road in what became the Abbey Foregate goods depot. These two had disappeared by about 1880. The engine houses of the other two companies were more substantial affairs and were built by Brassey. Both were three-road terminal sheds about 170ft long and 40ft wide built of brick under a slate hipped roof, and had tall round arched windows and a skylight the length of the building. The Shrewsbury & Chester's was built on the opposite side of its main line to the Castle Foregate goods depot, off Benbow Place, Coton Hill. It was a somewhat cramped site, reached by a single siding running south from the main line at the Ellesmere Road bridge, which led into a 50ft turntable just outside the entrance doors. The Locomotive Superintendent's offices were attached to the south end of the building.

The Shrewsbury & Hereford's shed was built in fields at Coleham, opposite its own goods depot. In 1855 the company decided to move its works to Shrewsbury after all, and by that summer had men working on the site extending the old engine house and building new workshops for locomotive repairs, carriage maintenance and also for wagon inspection. The main new building ran parallel to the first and was connected to it at one end by other buildings, giving the complex a square

horseshoe shape. This main extension was the workshop and had four tracks leading into it. The works were finished by January 1856 and must have been well laid out because the design was copied by the Cambrian Railways' Oswestry works soon after. When the Great Western and London & North Western took over the Shrewsbury & Hereford, after their joint lease of the line, the London & North Western took over the larger portion of the works at Coleham nearest to the main line and comprising the main workshops and offices. The Great Western took over the original shed and wagon shop, and the London & North Western was made to build a retaining wall to enable the Great Western's portion to be widened. The London & North Western seemed to have made the most use of the Coleham sheds, because in 1866 there were 51 engines stabled at the 'Salop Station', which was given the number 30 in the company's new shed code of the period. It was to keep this number until the London, Midland & Scottish changed the coding system in 1935, after which the shed became 4A.

The steady increase in traffic in the latter part of the 19th century meant a need for more locomotives and more shed room for them, and in 1877 the London & North Western demolished most of the old workshops on its side of Coleham and replaced them with a purpose-built 10-road shed of the company's standard pattern; a 50ft turntable was added at the side of the new building, and a coaling stage was built at around the same time. By 1912 there were 67 locomotives stationed at the company's Coleham shed. The only additions in London, Midland & Scottish days of any note were a larger (70ft) turntable, and then in the immediate postwar period a boiler house for the short-lived experiment in oil-fired engines was built near to the turntable by the firm of Leonard Faircloughs. It opened in 1947 but had soon closed when the oil-firing ceased and was adapted by the maintenance crew at the shed for stores.

The Great Western made relatively little use of Coleham at first, apart from using it for engines on the Severn Valley and Hereford

Top:
The old Engine House in Coton Hill, now a National Carriers Depot. *Author*

Above:
The LNWR side of the Coleham sheds, Shrewsbury, c1900. *Ian Allan Library*

lines. Instead it based most of its locomotives at the old shed off Benbow Place and built a new four-road through shed north of the Ellesmere Road bridge in what is now Coton Hill (North) yard. Exact details of this shed are somewhat sketchy; each lane had an inspection pit and there was a run-through coaling stage built alongside. The offices of the locomotive superintendents remained at the older shed, and the Great Western started building on Coleham at last in late 1882. A new standard Dean pattern roundhouse some 185ft square was added immediately to the south of the old Shrewsbury & Hereford shed, having 26 engine lanes radiating off a 50ft central turntable. It was opened in 1883, after which the shed in Coton Hill (North) seems to have been completely dismantled and disappears off the Ordnance Survey maps. The coaling stage survived a while longer, and the old shed off Benbow Place was still used for a time until being converted firstly into a fitting house and then into carriage workshops; later it was a warehouse of sorts and today it still survives, used by the lorry fleet of National Carriers Ltd.

Until 1897 Shrewsbury was head shed of its own district within the Northern Division, a district which stretched to Chirk on the Chester line, Ludlow on the Hereford, Buildwas on the Severn Valley line, Welshpool, Madeley Junction on the line to Wolverhampton, and included the branch lines in East Shropshire and the line from Wellington to Nantwich Junction. On official records up until 1918 it was simply abbreviated to 'SH', but after then it became coded 'SALOP', part of the Wolverhampton District; in the clerical codes of 1932 it became No 134 — the 13th shed alphabetically in the fourth (Wolverhampton) district. The only major change after Grouping was the transfer of the wagon repairs to Oswestry and the demolition of the wagon repair shops which were replaced by a new three-road shed of steel frames and corrugated sheeting in 1932. After Nationalisation, the two depots at Shrewsbury were amalgamated under the control of the Western Region and assumed the Code 84G. The transfer of the headquarters of the Cambrian section from Oswestry to Shrewsbury saw it recoded 89A on the first day of 1961, but within a short time the London Midland Region took over the shed and it was recorded yet again — this time as 6D. The shed was finally closed for steam on 5 March 1967 and by June 1970 was closed for diesels as well, although their visits had been increasingly rare and the shed served solely as a stabling point for them. The demolition of the site began in the early 1970s and all traces bar a fragment of office wall at the south end had gone by 1975.

The first locomotives to enter Shrewsbury were those on the Shrewsbury & Chester line. Under its locomotive superintendent Edward Jeffries the company had built up a good stock of 21 engines by 1849 and 34 by the time of the Great Western take-over. The first of these had been built by R. B. Longridges of Bedlington, Northumberland in 1846, being delivered in November and December of that year to work the North Wales Mineral section of the line prior to the extension to Shrewsbury. The first four engines had three different wheel arrangements but were all Stephenson's 'Long-Boilered' type. No 1 was a six-coupled goods engine with 4ft 9in wheels; Nos 3 and 4 had the same size driving wheels but were for mixed traffic use, being 2-4-0s. No 3 was a 2-2-2 fast passenger engine with 5ft 9in driving wheels. All had 15in × 24in cylinders. Nos 5 and 6 were similar engines with a 2-4-0 wheel arrangement, but had slightly smaller cylinders. All the long-boilered types tended to be unstable at speed, but this was not the cause of an accident at Rednal in 1865 in which No 5 left the tracks and many people were killed. The locomotive was withdrawn three years later. The other engines for the company came from a variety of builders including Bury, Curtis & Kennedy and the Sharp Brothers. There were a few oddities amongst the stock. In March 1853 the Vulcan Foundry of Newton-le-Willows supplied Nos 34 and 35, both 0-4-0s with exceptionally long wheelbases with 5ft 3in driving wheels and bar frames. Most of the engines were supplied new to the company but two were obtained second-hand, presumably

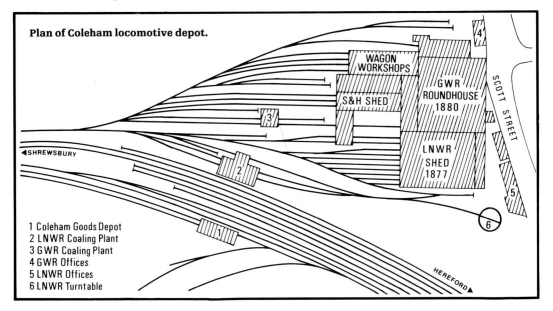

Plan of Coleham locomotive depot.

WAGON WORKSHOPS

GWR ROUNDHOUSE 1880

S&H SHED

LNWR SHED 1877

SCOTT STREET

◀SHREWSBURY

HEREFORD▲

1 Coleham Goods Depot
2 LNWR Coaling Plant
3 GWR Coaling Plant
4 GWR Offices
5 LNWR Offices
6 LNWR Turntable

for trials. One was called *The Wrekin*, of which virtually nothing is known apart from the fact it was acquired in 1852 and sold in 1853. The other was a 2-2-2 express passenger engine originally ordered by the Shrewsbury & Birmingham but acquired instead by the Chester company. This locomotive was built by the firm of Jones & Potts, Newton-le-Willows, in November 1852 and arrived at Shrewsbury at an unknown date to work expresses to Chester. It cost the then expensive sum of £2,000. Most of No 32's eccentrics and works, link motions and so forth were actually outside the frames, earning the locomotive the nick-name 'The Flying Flogger'. Only a handful of the Chester company's engines were given names officially, including Nos 13 and 21 which were named *Prince of Wales* and *Victoria & Albert* when they worked the Royal Train through from Chester to Shrewsbury and on to Wolverhampton in November 1852.

Although the Shrewsbury & Birmingham owned its locomotives the company paid the contracting firm of Johnson & Kinder to work them, with the contractors supplying everything from coal and lubricants, to engine drivers and clerks. When the company took over the running of its engines, in April 1853, Edmund Petre replaced William Marlow as locomotive superintendent briefly, before the stock was pooled with that of the Chester company under Joseph Armstrong. Locomotives began arriving before the line was ready and were stored at Shrewsbury by the Shrewsbury & Chester. A great deal of mystery surrounds the earliest engines ordered by the company, supplied by Stephenson's. There were four of them, all mixed-traffic 2-4-0s, but almost as soon as they had arrived they were sent back to the makers 'having proved very defective'. When they returned they were 0-4-2s, so whether Stephenson's replaced or rebuilt them is not really known. To make matters more confusing it turns out that the first engines were actually built at a factory near to the Stephenson's factory, under licence, unbeknown to the buyers.

The bulk of the company's other engines were supplied by Longridges in February and March 1849, being numbered 6-15. The first five of these were 0-4-2s with Stephenson Long Boilers, and with the exception of No 6 had 5ft driving wheels. No 6 had unusually small driving wheels just 4ft 4in, and was built mainly for shunting and light goods. As GWR No 40 she survived until 1904. The other Longridge engines were six-coupled goods engines, all with 4ft 9in driving wheels. As well as a few other 0-6-0s the company had four 2-2-2 express passenger engines. No 3 was one of the original batch from Stephenson's but does not appear to have been sent back like the others. She was named *Queen* after working the Royal Train in November 1852 with the Chester engines already mentioned. No 21 *Salopian* is said to have been the largest of the famous 'Jenny Lind' type of engines, and was built by Wilson's of Leeds in June 1849: this locomotive had 6ft 6in driving wheels. No 22 was a double-framed locomotive built by Fairburn, Williams & Co in November 1849 and was later given the name *Vulcan*.

Above left:
GWR No 5 (ex-Shrewsbury & Chester No 5), a 2-4-0 built in 1846 by Longridge; it was involved in the Rednal crash in 1865 and withdrawn three years after. *Real Photos*

Left:
GWR No 40 (ex-Shrewsbury & Birmingham No 6), which survived until 1904. *Real Photos*

No 23 *The Wrekin* was the last engine built by the famous firm of Bury, Curtis & Kennedy at its Clarence Foundry, Liverpool. The locomotive was 'painted in two coats of the best paint, finished with two coats of the best Copal varnish'; it had the standard buffers of the day, horsehair clad in leather. Delivered in July 1850, within days it had been involved in a collision with No 3 while standing at Shrewsbury station waiting to be put into service.

The locomotives were pooled in 1853 under the control of Joseph Armstrong; Jeffries had left in March of that year to take over the engines of the Shrewsbury & Hereford. Armstrong was already showing his talent in running his engines efficiently, and despite a great increase in locomotive requirements he actually managed to reduce significantly the cost per mile of each engine and improved their reliability. The amalgamation of the lines into the Great Western saw the Shrewsbury & Chester engines keep their numbers and the Shrewsbury & Birmingham ones having to change theirs; No 2 became No 36 and the rest were renumbered in sequence. No 1 was renumbered 33, inside the Shrewsbury & Chester's numbers, partly because of the pooling arrangements. With a few exceptions, all the Shrewsburies' engines were withdrawn by the late 1870s; Shrewsbury & Chester No 14 was withdrawn in December 1885 and was preserved for a time at Wolverhampton Stafford Works before tragically being cut up soon after World War 1.

Until the Shrewsbury & Hereford line was extended to Hereford, the company borrowed engines off the Shrewsbury & Chester to work the line. Jeffries arrived from that company in 1853 and set about ordering locomotives, and the first six 2-2-2s arrived between 1853 and 1854. Like the 'Flying Flogger' they were strange looking engines with outside workings and unusual link motion and very light frames. They were built by the Vulcan Foundry and numbered 1-6. The Vulcan Foundry also supplied other passenger engines later as well as seven 0-4-2 goods engines. Despite these, the company's Board in August 1854 complained to Brassey, the man running the line, of 'the great deficiency in the supply of engine power', and he was obliged to obtain some more. At the time he had been contracted to supply locomotives for a new railway in Canada and had built a factory in Birkenhead in which to do so. Between 1857 and 1861 four 2-2-2s, six 2-4-0s and three 0-4-2s, all of the 'Old Crewe' designs of the London & North Western, began arriving at Shrewsbury from Brassey's Canada Works. On the joint leasing of the line at the start of 1863 the locomotive stock, which had been bought from Brassey by the old company, was divided between the lessees. The London & North Western took all the 'Old Crewe' types built by Brassey along with another unknown engine. Apart from four new 0-6-0s just ordered, the Great Western let the West Midland Railway keep the rest.

The Shropshire Union and the Crewe lines were the preserve of the 'Old Crewe' designs of the London & North Western, although the records of which engine actually did work the lines have long since gone. Most work would have been done either by the Trevithick-Allan '6 foot' 2-2-2 Singles or the Allan '5 foot' 2-4-0 engines working passengers and goods respectively. At least one of each of these types found its way into the local papers. The accident that befell '6 foot' Single No 234 *Mazeppa* would have been funny it it had not had tragic consequences. *Mazeppa* was built at Crewe in 1849 and was working on the Stafford-Shrewsbury route in 1852. On 29 July it worked a local passenger train into Shrewsbury and when it booked into the Shropshire Union shed the driver reported a leaking regulator gland. The necessary packing repairs were carried out by the night fitter, Joseph Thompson, and the work was finished by the early morning. Thompson made up the fire in preparation for the locomotive's next duties and then left the shed at 5.50am, 10 minutes early. His day-time relief arrived at 6.10am, 10 minutes late. In the mean time *Mazeppa* had gone. A plateplayer raised the alarm after seeing an unmanned locomotive pass him near Belvidere, and another engine was sent off to chase the runaway. *Mazeppa* was finally stopped by the 6am morning train from Shrewsbury to Stafford as it stood at Donnington station; several of the carriages were wrecked in the collision and one of the passengers was killed. At the Inquiry it was learned that Thompson must have left the engine in gear, and as soon as steam had built up *Mazeppa* got moving. The engine survived the crash and was finally scrapped in 1878.

In March 1854 a 14-year-old youth was arrested for stealing about 40lb of the brasswork off 'the ballast engine *Python* belonging to the Shropshire Union company'. London & North Western No 69 *Python* was an Allan 2-4-0 goods engine built at Crewe in 1853. Apparently it had been standing for a few weeks in a siding near the Shropshire Union shed and the boy had stolen the

Above:

Not a PS&NWR engine, but one similar to three Manning Wardle 0-6-0Ts that did most of the work on the line up until 1880.

L&GRP courtesy David & Charles

brasswork for a 'fence' in the town. Although some surprise was expressed in court that he could have prised the brasswork off, he was found guilty.

The Welshpool and Minsterley lines were worked by the same 'Old Crewe' designs initially, but the Severn Valley line was worked by a variety of locomotives of the former Oxford, Worcester & Wolverhampton and Newport, Abergavenny & Hereford companies as well as those of the short-lived West Midland. Many of the engines were built by Hawthorn's or Kitson, mainly 2-2-2s and 2-4-0s. Slightly later two engines arrived from the Birkenhead Railway, Nos 30 and 31 built by Fairburns and renumbered as Great Western Nos 106 and 107. They worked the Severn Valley line for many years through several rebuilds and were finally withdrawn in 1900 and 1902.

The Potteries, Shrewsbury & North Wales had little money to spend on locomotives by the time its line was ready for opening, and had to buy three of France's contracting engines. These were all 0-6-0 tank engines with 3ft 10in wheels built by Manning Wardle in 1865 and were named *Powis*, *Sir Watkin* and *Bradford* (formerly *Viscount*); they provided the back-bone of the railway's locomotive power, working both passenger and mineral trains. Two small four-wheeled tank engines were also bought second-hand to work ballast trains. *Briedden* was a well tank engine supplied by Hawthorn's of Leith and had 3ft 8in solid wheels and occasionally worked light passenger trains. *Nantmawr* was built by

Hughes & Co of Loughborough in 1864 and had 3ft wheels and a saddle tank, and worked as the station yard pilot at Abbey station. Another tank engine, an 0-4-2 called *Tanat*, appears on the company records but little is known about it or from where it came. The official returns of 1866 show that there were 10 engines on the line in that year; the 1867 returns list seven engines. In December 1866 five engines were put up for sale so it would appear that just three actually went, and there are no records left of these locomotives. In July 1867 Mr Boulton of the famous 'Boulton's Sidings' went to Oswestry to pick up an 0-4-0 engine called *Dwarf*. Neither the Cambrian nor Great Western companies had such an engine, so could this have been one of the sold engines?

In 1872 the 'Potts' bought two locomotives; one was an ex-London & North Western Southern Division Bury 0-4-2 with 5ft driving wheels built in 1848 and originally numbered 34. By the time it arrived in Shrewsbury the locomotive had become No 1859 and kept that number during its short stay on the line. It was nicknamed 'Black Tom' by the company, though never officially named. The other engine was a new 2-4-0 tank engine built by the Yorkshire Engine Co of Sheffield and optimistically named *Hope*. In 1873 both

Above:
GWR No 30, one of the first engines built at Wolverhampton (in 1860) to replace withdrawn Shrewsbury & Chester locomotives. *Real Photos*

Right:
GWR No 219 in 1863. This 2-2-2 was originally Shrewsbury & Hereford No 5, built by the Vulcan Foundry. *Real Photos*

Nantmawr and *Briedden* were sold, followed soon afterwards by *Sir Watkin* and the two remaining mystery locomotives. From 1875 there were just four locomotives left — *Powis*, *Bradford*, *Tanat* and *Hope* — and after closure these were well looked after in the two-lane locomotive shed near the Abbey station in Shrewsbury before being sold off in the auction of 1888. In the minutes of the Shropshire Railway in September 1890 there is a reference for a scrap dealers bid for 'the two old engines now at the Abbey station'. These might have been older locomotives of the company withdrawn from service and so taken off the official returns, but all the voluminous records of the Potteries, Shrewsbury & North Wales Railway — which once filled an entire office with papers and deeds — have long since disappeared.

Having taken over its first sections of 'narrow gauge' line the Great Western set about building suitable locomotives to run along them. However, the Broad Gauge still took precedence over everything else and Armstrong had to fight to get his replacement engines. Swindon turned out its first standard gauge locomotives in May 1855, 12 double-framed six-coupled goods engines designed by Gooch and numbered 57-68. Several other types of 0-6-0 goods engines were turned out from Swindon, but the first of the passenger 2-2-2s were built by the new firm of Beyer Peacock & Co of Manchester in 1855; eight were built initially and numbered 69-76. They had 6ft 6in driving wheels and took over most of the passenger traffic on the main Wolverhampton-Shrewsbury-Chester line, and were

later transferred to work the early standard gauge passenger trains into Paddington. Beyer-Peacock also built several classes of 0-6-0s, all to Gooch's designs. The first locomotives turned out by the Stafford Road works in Wolverhampton were the 6ft Singles Nos 7 and 8 built to replace a pair of Shrewsbury & Chester engines in 1859, followed by a similar replacement in March 1860 — No 30. In 1862 George England & Co built eight 2-4-0s for stopping trains working north of Wolverhampton, with numbers 149-156.

Shrewsbury was to see most of the designs of Armstrong after he was promoted to Wolverhampton and later to Swindon. In 1865 he asked for 44 goods and eight passenger engines to work the increasing standard gauge

mileage. Few of the largest passenger classes found their way to Shrewsbury until the inauguration of the 'Zulu' expresses in 1880, when three of the 'Sir Daniel' class of 7ft Singles were stationed at Birkenhead to work the portion to and from Wolverhampton. Express locomotives began to be stationed permanently at Shrewsbury in 1888 with the start of the North-to-West expresses. On the route to London, locomotives were changed at Wolverhampton, not at Shrewsbury. On the North-to-West route the London & North Western locomotives handed over the trains to the Great Western engines at Shrewsbury. The England 2-4-0s Nos 149-152 were stationed at Shrewsbury; these had been rebuilt between 1878 and 1883 and were known as 'Chancellors'. In 1893 they were replaced by the new

Above:
**'360' class 0-6-0 No 367 was stationed at
Shrewsbury for several years to work local
goods traffic.** *Real Photos*

Below:
**'Bicycle' class 2-4-0 No 441 outside the coaling
plant at the GWR Coleham shed in the 1900s.**
Real Photos

Dean '3232' class of 2-4-0s but the expresses
had become too heavy for these engines and
they were replaced in turn by the new
'Badminton' class of 4-4-0s from 1898
onwards.

Other passenger trains on the Great
Western's lines were hauled by a variety of
engines including Armstrong's '806' class of
single-framed 2-4-0s from the 1870s, of which
Nos 806, 807, 810 and 821 were often to be seen
working between Wolverhampton and Chester,
and the 2-4-0 'Bicycles' of which Nos 439-443
were stationed at Shrewsbury for all types of
passenger work in 1902. The '3232' class
appeared in the middle of the 1890s to replace
the 'Sir Daniels' on the main line expresses,
and these were followed by more of the
'Badminton' 4-4-0s at the turn of the century.
Most of the goods work was carried on by the
0-6-0s of Beyer-Peacock, Armstrong and the
newer ones designed by Dean. The heavy coal
traffic from South Wales was hauled at first by
'79' and '330' classes, and then by the special
0-6-0s of the Armstrong '927' 'Coal Goods',
with local goods traffic and yard work handled
almost exclusively by 0-6-0 saddle tanks, the
forerunners of the famous panniers.

By 1902 Shrewsbury shed had three 'Atbara' 4-4-0s and a 'Badminton' — the latter aptly named *Shrewsbury* (GWR No 3307). Other engines seen prior to World War 1 included the heavy goods 2-6-0 'Aberdare' class designed for heavy coal traffic. In February 1912 four of the infamous 4-4-0 'County' class ('Rough-riders') arrived at Shrewsbury to take over the Shrewsbury-Bristol portion of the North-to-West trains; these were Nos 3820 *County of Worcester*, 3821 *County of Bedford*, 3822 *County of Brecon* and 3826 *County of Flint*, followed a month later by a fifth, No 3825 *County of Denbigh*. This was the first time Coleham shed had had a proper stud of modern express engines, and gradually the older types, which included some of the graceful Dean 4-2-2 Singles working out their

last years, were displaced. The war years saw the arrival of the first 4-6-0 'Saints' in the area as well as Churchward's '43xx' 2-6-0 mixed traffic engines, often put to work on passenger trains. In 1922 Shrewsbury had just two 'Saints', but 14 4-4-0s made up of four 'Counties', seven 'Dukes', two 'Atbaras' and

Above:
Forerunner of many 0-6-0PTs, an Armstrong '1016' class saddle tank, No 1070 was stationed at Shrewsbury at the turn of the century.
Ian Allan Library

Below:
One of the much-rebuilt Ramsbottom 'Lady of the Lake' 2-2-2 Singles, No 44 *Harlequin* at Coleham. In the background is the old Engine House, then used by the GWR. *Real Photos*

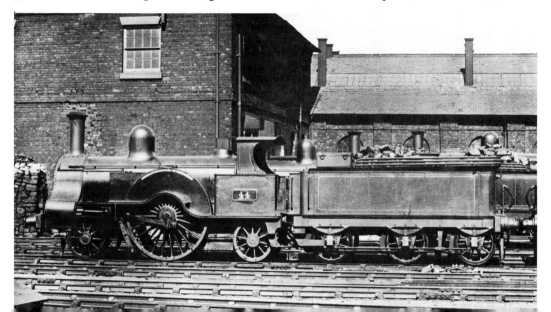

one 'City'. There were three of the '43xx' class, 13 0-6-0s (including some of the Beyer Peacock '322' class of 1864) and a large number of 0-6-0 and 0-4-2 tank engines.

For many years the 'Old Crewe' type of engines ran on the London & North Western lines in the area. In 1860 Stafford became the boundary between the Northern and Southern regions of the company so it is not unreasonable to assume that the vermillion red livery of the Southern Division was occasionally seen next to the green of the Northern at Shrewsbury — until Webb painted the whole lot black. The reign of Ramsbottom at Crewe saw the introduction of his 0-6-0 goods engines and the 2-4-0 passenger classes, but this was a gradual process as the London & North Western at this time was very conservative in outlook and never that bothered about the speed of its trains, especially local ones such as those working from Shrewsbury. By the time the 2-4-0 'Newtons' and 'Samsons' reached Shrewsbury they were getting fairly old. One Ramsbottom design that Shrewsbury saw a good deal of much later was his charming 'Lady of the Lake' class of 2-2-2 Singles. In the 1890s several were stationed at Shrewsbury to work local passenger traffic, and as late as 1896 five were stationed at Coleham. These were Nos 111 *Russell*, 117 *Tiger*, 612 *Princess Alice*, 804 *Soult* and 1435 *Fortuna*; all had been rebuilt twice by Ramsbottom's successor, Francis Webb.

The first Webb designs were simple and efficient and following the mid-1870s many of his '17in' 'Coal' 0-6-0 engines were to be seen working in and through Shrewsbury. These 'Coal' engines lasted for an amazingly long time hauling the heavy trains from Monmouthshire to the northwest and No 46 survived to be taken over by British Railways in 1948. Webb's other famous 0-6-0 was the '18' 'Crested Goods' known to all and sundry as 'Cauliflowers'. Whereas most of the 'Coal' engines worked through Shrewsbury, several 'Cauliflowers' were based there after the early 1880s to work local goods traffic. Like the 'Coal' engines, these survived in quite large numbers until Nationalisation. Together with Webb's rebuilt Ramsbottom 0-6-0s, the 'Special DXs', these Webb 0-6-0s made up the bulk of London & North Western goods engines up until the end of the century, along with his 0-6-2 'Coal Tanks' and other smaller tank engines mostly engaged on local goods and passenger traffic. In the 1890s the first of the eight-coupled Compound goods engines began to arrive to take over the heavier freight trains, and this basic design modified in turn

Below:
One of the short-lived 'John Hick' class of three-cylinder 2-2-2-2 Compounds, No 1548 *John Penn*, receives attention at the LNWR side of Coleham, c1900. *Real Photos*

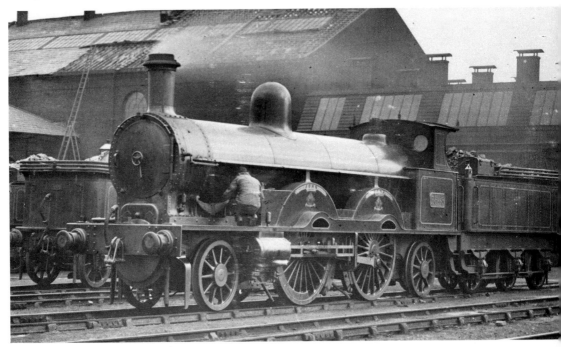

by Whale, Bowen-Cooke and Beames, was to carry on working this traffic up until World War 2 and the introduction of the Stanier '8Fs'.

Webb also built several designs of Simple 2-4-0s, the 'Precedents', 'Precursors', 'Whitworths' and the rebuilt Ramsbottom 'Newtons'; all the classes were very similar and the locomotives were usually just referred to as 'Jumbos' — with 6ft and 6ft 6in varieties. These initially handled the local traffic of the Shrewsbury area replacing older designs, but at the turn of the century Shrewsbury received allocations of almost brand new main line express locomotives. This was not, unfortunately, because of a change of policy by the company but to the dramatic failures of

Webb's experiments with compounding. He was given the position and had the power to carry out his plans for the ultimate express Compound, and although the new locomotives were theoretically brilliant, their performance never was, and their reliability was always suspect. They were quickly demoted to secondary duties such as the stopping trains on the Shrewsbury-Stafford and Shrewsbury-Hereford lines. Many of the failed three-cylinder Compound classes ended their days at Shrewsbury, including most of the 2-2-2-0 'Experiment' and 'Teutonic' classes and the 2-2-2-2 'Greater Britain' and 'John Hick' classes. Among the star engines at Shrewsbury was the one quite successful Compound,

Left:
GWR No 358 of the '322' class of 0-6-0s at Coleham c1905.
Real Photos

Below:
GWR Metropolitan Tank 2-4-0 No 5 was at Shrewsbury to work branch trains to Minsterley in the 1930s.
Real Photos

LNWR No 2062 *Herald* of the Webb 'Dreadnought' class of 2-2-2-0 three-cylinder Compounds at Shrewsbury in the early 1900s. *Real Photos*

'Teutonic' class No 1304 *Jeanie Deans* which had worked on the main 'Corridor' expresses from Euston to Crewe between 1891 and 1899. The 'John Hick' was probably the worst class of all, and the entire lot came to Shrewsbury; one of the class, No 1505 *Richard Arkwright*, was the last one to be scrapped, working its final days from Shrewsbury on local trains to Hereford up until 1912. Coleham shed seemed happy to have these prestigious, if useless, engines and they were kept in immaculate condition for the remainder of their short lives. After Whale took over the locomotive department at Crewe, the remaining Webb Compounds, the 4-4-0 four-cylinder variety, also found their way to Shrewsbury.

One other class of engine to be mentioned was far more successful; this was the class of 0-6-0 saddle tanks designed by Ramsbottom mainly for shunting and later rebuilt by Webb, who also built similar engines of the same type. Known as 'Screamers' on account of having an even higher pitched whistle than the other London & North Western engines, engines of this class worked the yards at Howard Street and at Coleham up until the 1930s. At the end of the day they would line up with their Great Western counterparts at the station, and rows of yard shunters and main line passenger engines of each company formed short but interesting trains waiting for the right of way to Coleham sheds.

After Webb's long-overdue departure from Crewe, Whale set about the radical rebuilding of the London & North Western's locomotive fleet and the new uncomplicated designs were soon seen in, and later based at, Shrewsbury. During Webb's time the Crewe-Shrewsbury line had become known as a good test track for engines new from the works or fresh from overhaul. It was built to a high standard and had several good expresses on it in connection with the North-to-West trains, but was not as busy as the other main lines from Crewe. Perhaps its use was also encouraged by the fact that it was often used by Webb on his visits to his country house near Craven Arms. The locomotive involved in the crash of 1907 was on a proving run after overhaul. The use of the line for testing engines has continued to this day and there is now a special rake of former passenger stock with mobile test units included on the working timetables, run daily by the Technical Department at Crewe. This rather eerie train has the carriage windows covered in with steel plates, but there has been little done to the rather tatty looking blue/grey livery. This latest train replaced a rake of

Above:
Whale's 'Precursor' class 4-4-0 No 365 _Alchymist_ at Coleham c1905. _Real Photos_

Below:
LNWR 0-8-0 goods locomotive No 1890 at Coleham c1905. _Real Photos_

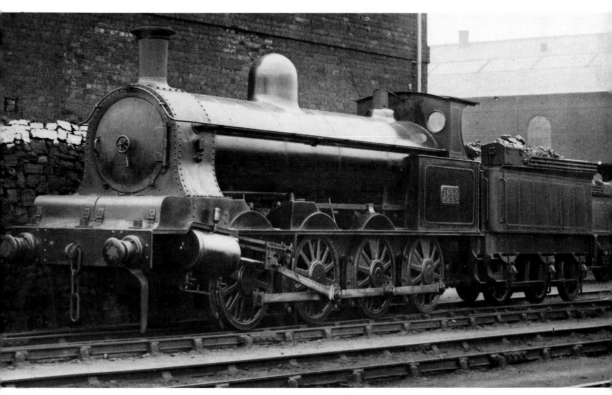

faded maroon carriages used previously up until the 1970s, but before then locomotives generally worked on revenue earning turns up until the end of the London, Midland & Scottish.

The new members of the 'Precursor' and 'Precedent' classes began to work the more important passenger trains as soon as the last of the failed Compounds departed. Most of the local passenger trains were in the more than capable hands of Webb's 0-6-2 tank engines, but these were supplemented by several Shrewsbury-based 'Jumbos'. The 0-6-2 tank engines had replaced the older tender engines on the Central Wales line towards the end of the century, but heavier trains needed more powerful engines and in 1911 Bowen-Cooke introduced his new class of 4-6-2 superheated tank engines that really made light work of the steep gradients on that line. Three were usually based at Shrewsbury for these trains, and occasionally they were to be seen running expresses from Shrewsbury to Crewe. In 1912

Shrewsbury was allocated a pair of 'Experiment' class 4-6-0s to work this portion of the North-to-West route, and there were also a few of the smaller-wheeled express goods version of a basically similar design, the '19in' Goods.

The Shropshire & Montgomeryshire was a typical Colonel Stephens railway and acquired its engines second-hand from a wide variety of places. For this line he did actually buy two brand-new locomotives and helped in their design himself. These were a pair of 0-6-2 tank engines built by Hawthorn, Leslie & Co and given the numbers and names No 5 *Pyramus* and No 6 *Thisbe*; true to form, they didn't last long as they were too heavy for the track and were sold. No 1 *Gazelle* must have been one of the most peculiar locomotives on the British railways. Built in 1893 by Dodman's of Kings Lynn, one of only two engines to be built in Norfolk, it weighed just over 4½ tons and was originally a 2-2-2 built for a local businessman for his private use. Stephens had it rebuilt by Bagnalls of Stafford as an 0-4-2 but retained the original well tank. Originally *Gazelle* worked the Criggion branch but later worked many excursions from Shrewsbury. The Army took it over to serve as an inspection train together with a rebuilt trailer. Originally it had

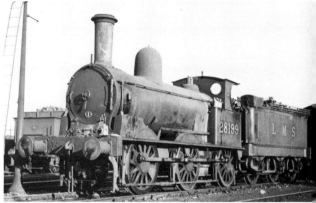

been coupled to an ex-LCC horse-drawn tramcar, but the bodywork of this was rotten by the time *Gazelle* was refurbished at Kinnerley in 1937. After World War 2 *Gazelle* was taken to Longmoor for preservation and is happily still with us; after a spell at the National Railway Museum in York the locomotive has now been transferred to the Army Museum on Humberside, though why it had to be moved away from York is unclear as the site would seem to be the best place for it (apart from back in Shropshire, of course!).

No 2 *Hecate* had a very dubious past. Although definitely not built for the Shrewsbury & Hereford line as often thought it was of great vintage nevertheless. It certainly had several characteristics of a Bury built engine, and was owned by the London & North Western before 1871. Stephens got the locomotive from a colliery in 1911 and by that time it was an 0-4-2 saddle tank. Renamed *Severn* in 1916 it was withdrawn in 1931 and like many other of the line's engines disintegrated gradually at Kinnerley. No 3 *Hesperus* was the pride of this motley collection and was chosen to work the first passenger trains. It was an

ex-London & South Western 'Ilfracombe Goods' 0-6-0 built by Beyer-Peacock in 1875, and Stephens seems to have paid for it on a form of hire purchase.

Following the departure of the two 0-6-2 tank engines, two further 'Ilfracombe' goods were acquired, taking their numbers and names as they replaced them in 1914 and 1916. The new No 5 *Pyramus* had been built in 1874 and the new No 6 *Thisbe* in 1873. In between the 'Ilfracombe' goods came an 0-6-0 saddle tank, No 4 *Morous*, built by Wardles of Leeds in 1866, and bought by Stephens in 1910. After World War 1 Stephens bought three ex-London, Brighton & South Coast 0-6-0T 'Terriers' from the War Stores Disposal Board: No 7 *Hecate* (Stephens seems to have liked this name) arrived in August 1921, and Nos 8 *Dido* and 9 *Daphne* in November 1923. None of these were particularly successful on the line and Nos 7 and 8 were withdrawn in 1930 followed shortly by No 9. They were cannibalised to repair other 'Terriers' on other Stephens lines, and *Daphne* was bought by the Southern Railways as this was cheaper than machining a new part for one of its ageing locomotives.

This motley collection of locomotives had difficulty enough in dealing with what little traffic there was, as there were seldom more than a couple capable of running at any one time in the 1920s. In March 1930 the company bought the first of three ex-London & North Western 'Coal' tanks, No 8108 of the London, Midland & Scottish, formerly LNWR No 2167 built in December 1874. In June 1931 came No 8182, built in December 1878, and soon after came No 8236, built in June 1881. Despite being as old as the engines they were replacing these three with *Hesperus* carried the brunt of the traffic from then on. Along with that engine and *Gazelle* they were the only ones on the line to be taken over by the Army in 1941 — and *Hersperus* was quickly scrapped. Before this time the aptly named Mr Funnel, in charge of the locomotive stock of the line, had lovingly

Below:
Whale 'Precursor' class 4-4-0 as LMS No 5280 at the ex-LNWR coaling plant, Coleham, in 1935.
L&GRP courtesy David & Charles

restored No 8108 and it emerged after nearly two years of work in resplendent 'Southern' green in May 1939, renumbered No 2. This splendour was to be short-lived and under Army control the locomotive reverted to its old number.

Between the wars Shrewsbury was a place of great interest to railway enthusiasts, a place where the London, Midland & Scottish met the Great Western, and where each displayed examples of locomotives ancient and modern; and there was always the side-show of the 'Potts' if there was nothing much happening at the General station. The London, Midland & Scottish relied heavily on former London & North Western engines, particularly in the 1920s, especially for goods traffic and local passenger work. Former main line express engines such as Whale's 4-4-0 were used on local stopping trains on the Shrewsbury-Stafford line until World War 2, and together with the later Bowen-Cooke 4-6-0 'Claughtons' worked the North-to-West trains north of Shrewsbury. Branch line traffic remained in the hands of Webb tanks, especially on the Ministerley branch where such engines remained until the passenger service stopped

Above:
No 6 *Thisbe* was one of the pair of 0-6-2 tank engines designed in part by Stephens for the Shropshire & Montgomeryshire. The locomotive proved too heavy for the line and was sold in 1916. *Real Photos*

Below:
S&MR No 2 *Hecate* was a locomotive with a mysterious past. It is seen here before its name was changed to *Severn* (in 1916). In the background one of the Stephens 0-6-2Ts is at work. *Real Photos*

Top right:

The 2-6-0 'Aberdare' class engines of the GWR were designed for heavy coal trains but were seldom stationed at Shrewsbury; here No 2660 stands outside the former Shrewsbury & Hereford shed at Coleham on 10 July 1938. The tender is off a scrapped ROD 2-8-0.
Peter Clay/LoS

Centre right:

GWR 'Star' class 4-6-0 No 4040 *Queen Boadicea* outside the GWR coaling plant at Coleham in the 1930s.
Real Photos

Below:

The streamlined Stanier Pacifics were certainly some of the more dramatic-looking engines of the 1930s. This is No 6220 *Coronation* standing at the north end of Shrewsbury station after a test run from Crewe in the late 1930s. *Real Photos*

in 1951, a real credit to the man who designed them. Most goods traffic (or freight as the London & Midland always called it) was still handled by six and eight-coupled engines whose designs also dated back to Webb, and many of the engines were built at Crewe when he was still in charge. Fowler rebuilt and re-designed several 0-6-0 classes, and other 'foreign' 0-6-0s from the constituent companies of the London, Midland & Scottish began to appear in the late 1920s, along with newer designs. Nevertheless, Webb's 'Coal' and 'Cauliflower' 0-6-0s still appeared in large numbers. For local passenger work Fowler designed a 2-6-4 tank which was introduced to Shrewsbury to work the Shrewsbury-Stafford, Shrewsbury-Welshpool and the Central Wales lines in particular. The occasional 'Royal Scot' or 'Patriot' 4-6-0 appeared on express trains from Crewe, usually on test runs.

The 1930s saw the arrival of the Stanier designs that changed the whole face of the company's locomotive stock, and the new Standard 2-6-0s, 4-6-0 'Black Fives' and 2-8-0s began to take the place of older locomotives, particularly in the late 1930s and after the war. More exotic locomotives appeared at Shrewsbury station straight from the works at Crewe — the famous 4-6-2s of the 'Princess Royal' and 'Duchess' classes and the exciting streamlined class-within-a-class, the 'Coronations'. These engines began to work on the North-to-West expresses to Crewe, along with

the 'Jubilee' 4-6-0s, but during the war began to look quite tatty, with external maintenance cut to a minimum. One surviving class in the period up to the war was the Ramsbottom 0-6-0 saddle tanks, still used for yard work until being replaced by more modern 0-6-0 tank engines such as the 'Jintys'. A rare visitor was the very occasional Beames 0-8-4 tank engine working on Shrewsbury-Swansea goods trains.

Most types of Great Western locomotive were to be seen at Shrewsbury at one time or another, with the exception of the 'King' class 4-6-0s which were not allowed to work north of Wolverhampton. The 1920s saw 'Castle' class 4-6-0s working on the Wolverhampton-Chester line with the main expresses, but most of this work was in the hands of the older 'Saints' and 'Stars' until the 1930s. The stopping trains on this route, and those working the Welshpool and Hereford lines, were usually hauled by the older 4-4-0s, and in 1922 Shrewsbury had four 'Bulldogs' and a 'Duke' to work these services. The Severn

Below:
The GWR borrowed several types of engines to replace engines borrowed off them by the Government, and LNER 'J25' 0-6-0 No 2071 was one of several allocated to Shrewsbury shed; it is seen here at Shrewsbury station on 21 June 1940. *Peter Clay/LoS*

Valley line was worked occasionally by one of the 4-4-0s, but more often by various classes of tank engines introduced for such traffic, including the Prairie tanks and the versatile 0-6-0 pannier tanks. Most goods traffic was still handled by 0-6-0s, mainly of the famous 'Dean Goods' variety but also of the newer Collett designs. Most of the ancient Beyer-Peacock '322' class had disappeared by the late 1920s. The Prairies and the Pannier tanks were also used extensively on smaller freight trains and there were rarer visits from the larger 2-8-2 tank engines on long distance goods to South Wales.

By the 1930s Shrewsbury was allocated many of the 'Star' class engines, and in 1932 had 11 of the class at one time mainly working the Shrewsbury-Bristol portion of the North-to-West expresses. The occasional 'Hall' or 'Manor' also made an appearance slightly later. One of the more versatile classes was the Moguls of Collett, the '43XX' class, of which Shrewsbury had a constant allocation of at least eight throughout most of the decade. On the longer distance and the express goods services, the main locomotives used were the '28XX' 2-8-0s, but these were not often allocated to Shrewsbury, and simply worked

through most of the time. World War 2 saw more of the main 4-6-0 classes with 'Castles' working many of the North-to-West trains south of Shrewsbury as well as the Wolverhampton-Chester portion of main line trains to and from Paddington. Shrewsbury had six 'Castles' in January 1943. 'Halls' took over some passenger work and also worked the longer distance goods trains, especially south of Shrewsbury. The war years saw some interesting locomotives on loan to the Great Western, following the departure of many of the 'Dean Goods' for war service at home and overseas. Shrewsbury was allocated three 'J25s' of the London & North Eastern Railway Nos 257, 536 and 2059. These were renumbered by the London & North Eastern when they were still at Shrewsbury, becoming Nos 5713, 5671 and 5710 respectively. They were returned in August 1946. The London & North Eastern also loaned a pair of its ROD 2-8-0s, designated by the company as the '04' class; there were Nos 6295 and 6336 and they were returned in early 1943. Among the other interesting arrivals on the Great Western were the American locomotives incorporated in the Lend-Lease arrangement. In January 1942 the first of four American Locomotive Co 2-8-0s arrived, No 1617, followed by Nos 1620 and 1622 in February and No 1615 in March. In June came No 1900, a similar design built by the Lima Locomotive Works, followed by Nos 1901 and 2375. All these were sent elsewhere by September 1944.

Once the Army had taken over the Shropshire & Montgomeryshire in 1941 it quickly realised that a drastic reinforcement of its locomotive stock was in order and borrowed locomotives from wherever it could. Two more 'Coal' engines were borrowed at first to supplement the three already on the line, as well as a succession of tank engines ranging from 0-6-0Ts of North Eastern Railway vintage to new 0-6-0Ts of the USA Transportation Corps; the American engines did not

Above left:
Once the Shrawardine Bridge had been rebuilt, the Army introduced the Austerity 0-6-0ST to replace the tender engines. WD75193 is seen here on the day of its arrival on the line.
Graham Vincent

Left:
Locally-made Sentinel engines were seldom allocated to Shrewsbury. One was usually allocated to the sub-shed at Ludlow to work the Clee Hill quarries, and No 47183 is seen on these duties in September 1950.
L&GRP courtesy David & Charles

Above:
Ex-LMS 4-6-0 'Royal Scot' class No 46169 *The Boy Scout* at Shrewsbury station in the early 1950s.
Russel Mulford/Michael Embrey

Below:
4-6-0 rebuilt 'Jubilee' class No 45735 *Comet* on the turntable at Coleham.
Russel Mulford/Michael Embrey

Left:
Changing times at Coleham, with a 'Black Five' 4-6-0 and a Brush Type 4 diesel on the turntable roads in the mid-1960s. On the left is the short-lived oil-firing plant built by the LMS.
Ian Allan Library

Below left:
Diesel power at Shrewsbury station on 12 June 1964. D374 heads a Swansea-Manchester train, and D1682 heads a Paddington-Birkenhead one.
Derek Cross

other 'Dukedogs' later. The Great Western type Railcars were used for a while on the Severn Valley line by the 1950s, but most passenger work on the line was handled by 2-6-2 tanks or 0-6-0 pannier tanks until the arrival of some British Rail Standard 2-6-4 tanks displaced from other services in the early 1960s. Most goods traffic was hauled by the pannier tanks. Other Great Western locomotives included the Collett 0-6-0 and 2-6-0 classes that had been there since before the war and were to last almost to the last years of steam. 'Kings' were finally allowed on the line up from Hereford in 1951 and in February of that year No 6000 *King George V* made its first run on the long double-home Newton Abbot-Shrewsbury turn. The 'Kings' were never that common on the route, and only began to arrive in Shrewsbury in numbers after they had been passed for running north of Wolverhampton, and they were being displaced by diesel traction elsewhere. For the most part, Great Western type locomotives stayed at 'their' side of the Coleham sheds.

At the other side of the sheds were the London Midland engines, largely based of course on London, Midland & Scottish designs. Stanier had completely changed and standardised the old company, and the main passenger and goods trains south of Shrewsbury were hauled mostly by his 4-6-0 'Black Fives', with the 2-8-0s dealing with the heavier goods traffic. Much of the local passenger traffic to Stafford and to Welshpool was still dealt with by the Fowler 2-6-4Ts but these were displaced on the Central Wales line by the 1950s and replaced by 'Black Fives' as well. The most interesting locomotive turns were still those to Crewe with the North-to-West trains hauled by anything from 'Baby Scots' to 'Duchesses' and, after the introduction of British Railways Standard classes, 'Britannia' Pacifics. Gradually the former London, Midland & Scottish express classes worked south of Shrewsbury as well, followed by the 'Britts'. On 7 February 1962 No 46220 *Coronation* became the first, and only one, of her type to use the Severn

last long. By far the most successful engines on the line were the requisitioned 'Dean Goods' which took the bulk of the works and ammunition trains right up until 1948. Some were fitted with special pannier tanks to supplement the water carried in their tenders, and some also had their cab roofs extended to help with the black-out conditions. After the Shrawardine Bridge was strengthened in 1948 the 'Austerity' 0-6-0 saddle tanks took over virtually all the traffic on the line until closure, and many of the 'Dean Goods' stood alongside the 'Coal' engines in the sidings at Hookagate for a long time before being taken away for scrapping; some were actually scrapped on the spot.

Nationalisation followed the war and the last decades of steam running saw the usual wide variety of engines at Shrewsbury. By 1946 the last Great Western passenger design, Hawksworth's 'County' class 4-6-0s, were running between Wolverhampton and Chester, along with 'Castles', the few remaining 'Stars', and the 'Halls'. Three 4-4-0s — two 'Dukes' and one of the hybrid '90XX' 'Dukedogs' — were still allocated to Shrewsbury to work trains on the Welshpool and Severn Valley line, but these had soon gone only to be replaced by

Above:
Diesel multiple-units wait in the sidings south of Shrewsbury station in April 1982. *Author*

Left:
Until recently, Class 40 locomotives were regular visitors to Shrewsbury on heavier goods workings. No 40.080 heads a ballast train bound for Bayston Hill in July 1982. *Author*

Tunnel on a turn from Shrewsbury to Bristol. There were still a great number of 0-6-0 engines on goods work as well as several classes of 2-6-2Ts on goods and light passenger work. The British Railways Standard classes continued to arrive in considerable numbers and by 1965 Shrewsbury had been allocated 15 of the '5MT' 4-6-0s. Oddly enough some of these engines were replaced earlier, in 1960, by a stud of six 'Jubilees', engines that had seldom before been allocated to Shrewsbury.

The first few diesels to arrive in Shrewsbury (apart from short-lived trials with small 0-4-0 shunters on the 'Potts' in the war years) were standard 0-6-0 shunters which arrived in the late 1950s. The Western Region introduced its diesel-hydraulic classes briefly on Paddington-Birkenhead trains in the early 1960s, with the 'Westerns' working north of Wolverhampton for a year or so after 1962. Later they also worked on the Hereford line, as did the occasional 'Warship' diesel on through turns from the southwest to Crewe. These locomotives were also tried on the line from Birmingham. The 'Hymeks' also worked to and through Shrewsbury on goods trains and the occasional passenger turn, but all these classes were frowned upon by the London Midland after it took over the area in 1963 and began to be seen increasingly rarely. The odd 'Western' was still to be seen on a goods or special passenger duty until the early 1970s, and the 'Hymeks' were often used to take trains of rails from Hookagate to the Western Region.

Above:
A Wolverhampton train waits in Bay No 5 at Shrewsbury on 27 March 1985, with a twin-car Central Wales train in the adjacent No 6 platform. *Author*

Right:
Since the demise of Coleham sheds most visiting locomotives to Shrewsbury are put into a siding near the Gay Meadow ground of Shrewsbury Town FC, where solitary Class 47 No 47.217 waits on 27 March 1985. *Author*

The London Midland introduced its own diesel-electrics after about 1964, notably the Brush Type 4s (Classs 47) and the Type 2s (Class 24/25); most steam working of main line passenger trains ceased in 1965 and was only re-introduced in emergencies. For the end-of-the-main-line trains from Paddington in March 1967 steam-haulage was brought back, with 'Black Five' No 45116 hauling the last Paddington-Birkenhead train through Shrewsbury on 4 March; on the same day the last steam-hauled train through to the Welsh coast on the Welshpool line was the 'Cambrian Coast Express', hauled by Standard Class 4 No 75033 on the up train to Shrewsbury, and by No 75021 on the return. Ian Allan Ltd ran two specials at this last weekend, using *Pendennis Castle* and *Clun Castle*. Of the few locomotives of Great Western origin kept on by the London

Midland almost up until the end of steam, most were 'Manors' displaced from Oswestry shed with the closure of some of the Cambrian sections. The occasional '9F' 2-10-0 worked south from Crewe or from Birkenhead to Coton Hill yard until the closure of Birkenhead and Crewe (South) sheds in November.

The Western Region had put its cross-country diesel multiple-units on the Hereford line after that was rationalised, complete with mini-buffet at times. These were replaced by the London Midland with its own units. A plan by the Western Region to use railcars with trailers on the Welshpool line and on to the

coast was stopped by the transfer of the line to the London Midland, as its multiple-units could not take trailers. By the early 1970s the shortened North-to-West route was only a Crewe-Cardiff cross-country affair served by DMUs but locomotive-hauled trains were introduced, from start of the 1980s using Class 33s off the Southern Region that are still officially based at Eastleigh, and have to 'work their passage' south to get repairs and overhauls carried out. Class 47s now dominate the through trains to London (Euston), handing over to electric engines at Wolverhampton. Since the demise of the English Electric Type 40s, formerly a familiar part of the Shrewsbury scene, heavy goods traffic has been mainly worked by Class 37 and Class 47 locomotives, supplemented by the rapidly dwindling ranks of Class 25 locomotives. Class 37s also took over from Class 25s, double-heading the Summer Saturday Aberystwyth services in 1985 from Shrewsbury. Rarer visitors are the Class 45 'Peaks' and the newer Class 56s which have appeared since the mid-1980s. Locomotive haulage on regular passenger trains was extended to Chester in 1984, and will be extended to Aberystwyth soon with through trains from London in the summer timetables on a daily, rather than Saturdays only, basis. The ageing DMUs working on all stopping trains radiating from Shrewsbury are finally due to be replaced by the Class 151 'Sprinters' by 1986-87.

Since 1972 Shrewsbury has again thrilled to the beat of steam engines as the line to Newport was passed for steam working by British Rail, and *King George V* returned to the town on 16 September. Since then steam running has been extended to Chester, making this route the longest, and many of the famous preserved engines have appeared on these runs.

Top left:
The shape of things to come — Class 56s have been seen more frequently in the last year or so. Here 56.104 stands at Shrewsbury in the bitter cold of February 1985. *Author*

Bottom left:
The driver of Class 25 No 25.048 chats with the Sutton Bridge Junction signalman in July 1982. *Author*

Below:
Coton Hill yard on 25 March 1985; Class 08 shunter No 08.686 takes a rest from shunting, while Class 25 No 25.044 sits at the head of a train of empty ballast wagons. *Author*

Appendix — Locomotive Allocations

Great Western Railway: Shrewsbury (Salop) January 1902

4-4-0s
Nos 3307 *Shrewsbury*; 3391 *Wolseley*; 3398 *Colombo*; 3401 *Gibraltar*.

2-4-0s
Nos 12; 152; 156; 198; 210; 439; 441; 442; 443; 834; 1443.

0-6-0s
Nos 366; 367; 369; 396; 403; 419; 423; 516; 687; 689; 702; 709; 1092; 1110.

2-2-2s
No 30.

0-6-0STs
Nos 1504; 1783; 1917; 1986; 2711.

2-4-0Ts
No 3519.

0-4-2Ts
No 532.

Total: 37 locomotives.

Great Western Railway: Shrewsbury (Salop) January 1912

4-4-0 'Badminton' class
Nos 3301 *Monarch*; 3307 *Shrewsbury*; 3309 *Shakespeare*; 3311 *Wynnstay*.

4-4-0 'Atbara' class
No 3403 *Hobart*.

4-4-0 'City' class
No 3434 *City of Birmingham*.

2-4-0 'Bicycle' class
Nos 439; 440; 441; 442.

2-4-0s
Nos 718; 722.

2-2-2s
Nos 30; 110.

0-6-0s
Nos 58 (1855); 65 (1855); 87 (1857); 317 (1965); 334 (Beyer-Peacock '322'); 335 (Beyer-Peacock '322'); 359 (Beyer-Peacock '322'); 361 (Armstrong '360'); 363 (Armstrong '360'); 364 (Armstrong '360'); 408 (Armstrong '360'); 419; 683; 705 (Armstrong '388'); 928; 1089 (Armstrong '388').

0-4-2T Armstrong '517' class
Nos 517; 836; 1427.

2-4-0T 'Metropolitan Tanks'
No 1445.

0-6-0STs
Nos 1505; 1742; 1801; 1951; 1988; 2961.

0-4-2STs
No 1082.

Total: 41 locomotives.

London & North Western Railway: Shrewsbury (Code 30) 9 November 1912

4-6-0 'Experiment' class
Nos 1074 *City of Dublin*; 2022 *Marlborough*.

4-6-0 '19in' 'Goods' class
Nos 1350; 2508; 2593.

4-6-0 'Compound Goods'
No 1400.

4-4-0 'Jubilee' 7ft Compounds
Nos 1906 *Robin Hood*; 1928 *Hatton*.

4-4-0 'Benbow' 7ft Compounds
Nos 1956 *Illustrious*; 1959 *Revenge*; 1963
Boadicea; 1965 *Charles H. Mason*; 1970 *Good
Hope*; 1972 *Hindustan*.

2-4-0 'Precedent' class (6ft 6in Jumbo)
Nos 364 *Pease*; 864 *Pilot*; 869 *Llewellyn*.

2-4-0 'Whitworth' class (6ft Jumbo)
Nos 401 *Zeno*; 628 *Tartarus*; 885 *Vampire*.

0-8-0 'B' Compounds
Nos 640; 1230; 2561.

0-8-0 'C' Simples
No 2529.

0-8-0 'C1' Simples
Nos 1841; 2534.

0-8-0 'D' Simples
Nos 1815; 1821; 1824; 2527; 2547.

0-8-0 'G' Simples
No 1322.

0-6-0 'Special DX' class
Nos 3045; 3066; 3076; 3179; 3206.

0-6-0 '18in Goods' class
Nos 59; 339; 467; 533; 725; 727; 776; 1702;
1712; 2332.

0-6-0 'Coal' class
Nos 108; 851.

4-6-2T Superheated Tanks
Nos 217; 375; 1366.

0-6-2T '18in Tanks'
Nos 586; 1032; 2113.

0-6-0ST 'Specials'
Nos 264; 525; 3120; 3219; 3374; 3381.

2-4-2T 5ft 6in Tanks
Nos 187; 199; 402.

2-4-0T 4ft 6in Tanks
No 999.

0-4-0ST 4ft Tanks
Nos 3033; 3070; 3241.

Total: 68 locomotives.

Great Western Railway: Shrewsbury (Salop) 1 January 1932

4-6-0 'Star' class
Nos 4003 *Lode Star*; 4021 *The British Monarch*;
4027 *The Norwegian Monarch*; 4028 *The
Roumanian Monarch*; 4038 *Queen Berengaria*;
4041 *Prince of Wales*; 4046 *Princess Mary*;
4053 *Princess Alexandra*; 4062 *Malmesbury
Abbey*.

4-4-0 'Bulldog' class
Nos 3306 *Armorel*; 3352 *Pendragon*; 3366 *Earl
of Cork*; 3414 *A. H. Mills*.

4-4-0 'Duke' class
No 3273 *Mounts Bay*.

4-6-0 'Saint (Court)' class
No 2939 *Groome Court*.

4-6-0 'Hall' class
No 5916 *Trinity Hall*.

2-6-0 '43XX' class
Nos 4332; 4338; 4539; 5346; 6303; 6320; 6342;
7317.

2-6-0 'Aberdare' class
No 2671.

2-8-0 ROD class
No 3033.

0-6-0 'Dean Goods'
Nos 2322; 2348; 2359; 2389; 2442; 2444; 2464;
2477; 2488; 2579.

0-6-0ST/PT Armstrong '1016' class
Nos 1045; 1075.

0-6-0ST/PT Dean '655' class
No 1783.

0-6-0ST/PT Dean '850' class
Nos 857; 865; 1947; 2004; 2005; 2010.

0-6-0ST/PT Dean '2021' class
Nos 2028; 2061.

2-4-0T '455 Metropolitan Tank' class
No 5.

Total: 48 locomotives.

British Railways (Western Region): Shrewsbury (84G) 1950

4-6-0 'Star' class
Nos 4040 *Queen Boadicea*; 4044 *Prince George*; 4046 *Princess Mary*; 4052 *Princess Beatrice*; 4061 *Glastonbury Abbey*.

4-6-0 'Castle' class
Nos 5032 *Usk Castle*; 5050 *Earl of St Germans*; 5061 *Earl of Kirkenhead*; 5064 *Bishops Castle*; 5073 *Blenheim*; 5086 *Viscount Horne*; 5097 *Sarum Castle*; 7035 *Ogmore Castle*.

4-6-0 'Hall' class
Nos 4904 *Binnegar Hall*; 4919 *Donnington Hall*; 5981 *Frensham Hall*; 5994 *Roydon Hall*; 6963 *Throwley Hall*; 6976 *Graythwaite Hall*; 6980 *Llanrumney Hall*.

4-6-0 Stanier '5MT' class
Nos 44835; 44908; 45112; 45143; 45145; 45180; 45183; 45190; 45245; 45281; 45283; 45298; 45318; 45330; 45384; 45400; 45406; 45422; 45436.

2-6-0 '43XX' class
Nos 6307; 6338; 6348; 7319.

2-8-0 '28XX' class
No 2841.

2-8-0 Stanier '8Fs'
Nos 48207; 48307; 48308; 48328; 48347; 48369; 48373; 48474; 48478; 48688.

2-8-0 'War Department' class
Nos 90110; 90113; 90123; 90366; 90535; 90548; 90561.

0-8-0 '7F' (ex-LNWR designs)
Nos 48901; 48945; 49138; 49276; 49440.

0-6-0 Collett '2251' class
Nos 2228; 2229; 2231; 2233; 2234; 2235; 3217.

0-6-0 '3F' (ex-Midland Railway)
Nos 43357; 43394; 43570; 43581; 43600; 43679; 43757; 43760.

0-6-0 '3F' (ex-Lancashire & Yorkshire Railway)
Nos 52414; 52428; 52525; 52551.

0-6-0 '2F' (ex-Midland Railway)
Nos 58211; 58213; 58322; 58327; 58330; 58333.

2-6-2T '51XX' class
Nos 4118; 5154; 5168.

2-6-2T '3MT' Fowler class
Nos 40005; 40008; 40048; 40048.

0-6-2T '56XX' class
Nos 5642; 5673; 6606; 6633; 6683.

0-6-2T Webb Coal Tank (ex-LNWR)
Nos 58881; 58904.

0-6-0PT '2721' class
No 2744.

0-6-0PT '57XX' class
Nos 3602; 3702; 3782; 3788; 4602; 4623; 4672; 9656; 9657; 9672; 9719.

0-6-0T '1F' class (ex-Midland Railway)
No 41725.

0-4-0T Sentinel
No 47183.

0-4-0ST 'OF' 'Pug' (ex-Caledonian)

No 56027.

Total: 120 locomotives.

British Railways (London Midland Region): Shrewsbury (6D) 1965

4-6-0 'Manor' class
Nos 7801 *Anthony Manor*; 7802 *Bradley Manor*; 7812 *Erlestoke Manor*; 7819 *Hinton Manor*; 7822 *Foxcote Manor*; 7827 *Foxcote Manor*; 7828 *Odney Manor*.

4-6-0 '5MT' BR Standard class
Nos 73000; 73025; 73034; 73035; 73036; 73050; 73053; 73067; 73070; 73071; 73090; 73094; 73095; 73097; 73167.

4-6-0 '4MT' BR Standard class
Nos 75014; 75038; 75053; 75063.

2-6-0 '2MT' Ivatt class
Nos 46510; 46511; 46519.

2-8-0 Stanier '8F' class
Nos 48122; 48345; 48404; 48418; 48436; 48471.

2-6-4T '4MT' BR Standard class
Nos 80048; 80100; 80135; 80136.

2-6-2T '2MT' Ivatt class
Nos 41207; 41209; 41304.

0-6-0PT '57XX' class
Nos 3709; 3754; 9657.

Diesel 0-6-0 Shunters
D3111; D3193; D3194; D3970.
Total: 49 locomotives.